P9-BYN-821

THE COLD WAR

TOP
SECRET
FILES

TOP SECRET FILES

THE COLD WAR

STEPHANIE BEARCE

PRUFROCK PRESS INC.
WACO, TEXAS

Library of Congress Cataloging-in-Publication Data

Bearce, Stephanie.
 Top secret files : the Cold War : secrets, special missions, and hidden facts about the
CIA, KGB, and MI6 / by Stephanie Bearce.
    pages cm
 Includes bibliographical references.
 ISBN 978-1-61821-419-5 (pbk.)
 1. Espionage--History--20th century--Juvenile literature. 2. Spies--Juvenile literature. 3.
Cold War--Juvenile literature. I. Title. II. Title: Cold War, secrets, special missions, and
hidden facts about the CIA, KGB, and MI6.
 UB270.5.B415 2015
 327.1209'045--dc23
                                            2015006674

Illustrations by Zachary Hamby on pages 15, 16, 29, 33, 36, 40, 47, 52, 71, 75, 76, and 86.

Edited by Lacy Compton

Cover and layout design by Raquel Trevino

ISBN-13: 978-1-61821-419-5

Printed in the United States of America.

At the time of this book's publication, all facts and figures cited are the most current
available. All telephone numbers, addresses, and website URLs are accurate and active.
All publications, organizations, websites, and other resources exist as described in the
book, and all have been verified. The author and Prufrock Press Inc. make no warranty
or guarantee concerning the information and materials given out by organizations or
content found at websites, and we are not responsible for any changes that occur after
this book's publication. If you find an error, please contact Prufrock Press Inc.

Prufrock Press Inc.
P.O. Box 8813
Waco, TX 76714-8813
Phone: (800) 998-2208
Fax: (800) 240-0333
http://www.prufrock.com

Table of Contents

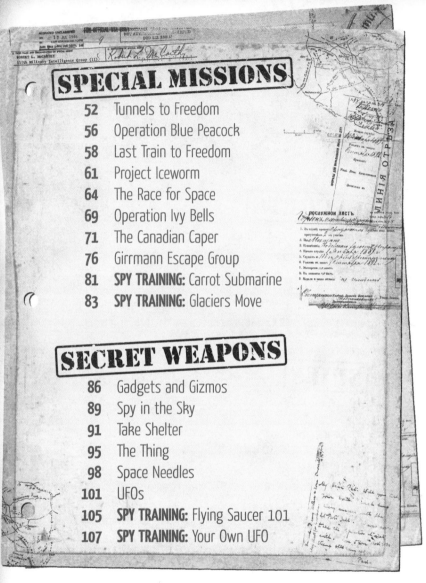

Secrets

TOP SECRET

South Korean Army Cold War soldiers from Camp Ashworth, 1964

Two U.S. Army officers talk with two soldiers at a Nike missile battery, 1950s

FIRST

LIGHTNING

TOP SECRET

It was pitch dark when they started setting up for the test. The test tower stood tall and black, waiting for the fully assembled bomb to be loaded. At 2 a.m. on August 29, Igor Kurchatov ordered the bomb to be wheeled to the tower. By 6 a.m., everything was ready. The Soviet Union was going to test its own nuclear bomb.

The project was called First Lightning and had been in the works since WWII. The Soviets had planted spies in the

American Manhattan project and had managed to steal the plans for the atomic bomb. That's why the bomb looked so similar to the American weapon.

The Soviet scientists had meticulously prepared the test site. They had constructed buildings out of brick and wood to simulate office buildings and homes. They had built bridges, tunnels, and water towers. They had even set up an area similar to a small farm with animals like cows and chickens. It was all a part of the test. They wanted to see what the effects of the blast would be on the buildings and animals.

At promptly 6 a.m., the countdown began. Within seconds, First Lightning exploded in an unbearably bright blaze. White-hot fire engulfed the launch tower. The buildings and animals were obliterated by a giant fireball rising up into the sky and forming a huge mushroom-shaped cloud. The 20-kiloton explosion could be seen from 9 miles away. It was a total success.

It was also the start of an arms race between the United States and the Soviet Union. Each country was afraid that the other would use the nuclear bomb to obliterate its enemy. Neither country wanted to unleash that devastation on the world, but felt pressured to build bigger and better weapons to protect themselves in the event of a war. Neither side ever launched a full-scale attack—therefore it was called a cold war, and it would last for nearly 40 years.

The seeds of the Cold War were planted long before the start of World War II. Two large countries, the United States of America and the Soviet Union, did not trust each other. The two countries had very different governments. The United States believed in a capitalist system, where individual people owned businesses and land and received the profits of their work. The Soviet Union believed in communism, where the government owned the businesses and land and citizens received their homes, food, and income from the government.

But despite their very different governments, they did agree that Nazi Germany had to be stopped. So they became allies for World War II and both countries fought to stop Germany. However, even while they were fighting together, they still did not trust each other—both sides kept secrets and spied on each other.

One big secret that the United States did not want to share with the Soviet Union was the Manhattan Project and its plans for a nuclear bomb. Leaders in the U.S. and Britain believed that if Russia learned how to build a nuclear bomb, then it might someday use it on Europe or even the United States. Both President Roosevelt and President Truman refused to explain anything about the weapon they were building to the Russians. This secrecy made the Soviet leader, Joseph Stalin, furious. He planted spies in the Manhattan Project so that he could learn the secrets of nuclear technology. This in turn made the Americans furious.

Klaus Fuchs was a scientist who had worked on the Manhattan Project. He agreed to spy for Stalin and handed over information that helped the Soviet Union begin secret work on its own bomb.

When America and Europe learned about the Soviet Union's successful testing of First Lightning, they were frightened. They were afraid that the Soviet Union would use its new weapon to start another war, take over more land in Europe and spread communism, or possibly attack the United States. The Soviet Union argued that it had to develop its own atomic bomb to protect itself from the United States.

Neither of the countries wanted to launch nuclear weapons at each other. They had seen the horrible effects that the bombs had on the people of Japan. But the countries didn't trust each other either.

The United States, Britain, France, and eight other democratic countries formed a group called the North Atlantic Treaty Organization (NATO). These countries agreed to a system of mutual defense, where if one of the countries was attacked, then all of the countries would help defend it.

The communist countries near the Soviet Union formed their own group called the Warsaw Pact. These eight countries, including East Germany, Czechoslovakia, and the Soviet Union also agreed to defend each other if one of them was attacked.

For the next 40 years, the NATO countries and those in the Warsaw Pact fought a cold war. They did not send soldiers to fight the war or drop bombs, but they sent spies to learn each other's secrets. They stole plans for each other's weapons and raced to see who could build the biggest army and the fastest weapons, and who could get into space first. It was a war that was fought by secret agents from the KGB, the CIA, and MI6. It was a war of secrets—the winner would be the side that could keep its secrets safe, while stealing the secrets of the other countries.

The Beard

While nuclear scientist **Igor Kurchatov** was working on the Soviet nuclear bomb, he vowed he would not cut his beard until the program was a success. He grew a long bushy beard and continued to wear the beard even after the successful tests. He liked to cut his beard into unusual styles. Friends and colleges gave him the nickname, "The Beard."

Gene Grabeel stared at the papers on her desk. They were gibberish. Pages full of nothing but random letters, numbers, and spaces. But it was supposed to be a code. A Soviet code that nobody could figure out.

Just a few weeks before she was assigned to Arlington Hall, VA, Gene had been a busy schoolteacher. But with the war raging across Europe, Gene had decided to volunteer for the U.S. Army Signal Security Agency. In 1943, the SSA was in charge of intelligence and spy activities, and Gene had just been assigned to the Venona project. It was a project that would last for 40 years.

During WWII, the Soviet Union fought with America and Britain against the Nazis, but Carter W. Clarke, a U.S. Army intelligence officer, didn't trust Joseph Stalin. He was sure that Stalin was trying to steal plans for allied weapons and equipment. He selected a small group of code breakers and assigned them the job of breaking the Soviet Code. They had to keep their work even more secret than the people working to break the German and Japanese ciphers, because the Soviets were supposed to be one of the Allies. If the Soviets found out that the United States was trying to break their codes, it could change their allegiance.

It took 3 years before cryptanalysts were able to crack the code. It was incredibly complex because the Soviets used a one-time pad system. This meant that the person sending the code was using a code book with randomly generated letters and numbers. The "book" was a printed pad of paper and once the top sheet had been used, it was torn off and destroyed. The

The OOOOOOOOh No Code!

Codes are supposed to be as secure as possible. Experts warn that even your computer passwords need to be tricky and hard for someone else to guess. But during the Cold War, the secret unlock code for the Minuteman missile was 00000000. For nearly 15 years, the U.S. government had a code that was easy to crack on this very deadly missile. Good thing the Soviet Union didn't find out! (And good thing the U.S. had several other safeguards in place!)

pad was so small it could fit in the palm of an agent's hand and had to be read with a magnifying glass.

If the Soviets had used the pad correctly, then it would have been impossible for the Venona team to break their code. But the Soviets got sloppy and sometimes reused the same code sheet. It was this simple mistake that allowed Lieutenant Richard Hallock to decipher a few words. But it wasn't until after the end of the war in December of 1946 that the code breakers were able to make sense of the messages. When they finally broke the code, the Venona team learned that Chief Clarke was right. The Soviets were spying and had even had spies on the Manhattan Project. The Soviets had managed to steal the American plans for the atomic bomb.

The Venona team was shocked to discover the identities of numerous spies placed in high government jobs in America, Canada, Britain, and Australia. There were spies in the State Department in Washington, DC, the Treasury, and even in the White House.

The Venona Project discovered the Soviet code names for hundreds of people and places. For example:

» Kaptain: President Roosevelt
» Babylon: San Francisco
» Arsenal: U.S. War Department
» Enormoz: Manhattan Project (atomic bomb)

The leaders of the Allied countries were shocked at the extent to which they had been infiltrated by Soviet spies. This new knowledge helped them arrest and prosecute some spies, but it also made them increase their own spy programs. If the Soviet KGB was going to spy and steal information, the United States and its allies needed to increase their own espionage activities. And the Soviets could not suspect how the United States had learned its secrets. Project Venona would have to stay a secret until the end of the Cold War.

They Built a Wall

It was an ordinary Saturday in Berlin. People in the divided city did what they had been doing since the end of WWII. They visited friends and families in all parts of the city. Sure, the people from East Berlin had to show a pass to get into West Berlin, and West Berliners did the same to go to the east side. But nobody stopped them.

They went to birthday parties for cousins and had family picnics at the park. They visited the theatres in East Berlin and had supper in the West Berlin restaurants. At the end of the evening, boyfriends and girlfriends said good night and went home to opposite sides of the city. Aunts and uncles, grandparents and siblings said "Auf Wiedersehen," and school friends said "bis später." No one thought that the next day would be any different.

But at one minute past midnight on Sunday, August 13, a secret mission, "Operation Rose," was put into action by the leaders of East Germany. Hundreds of East German soldiers arrived at the borderline between East and West Berlin. They began digging up the roads and tearing down bridges. They put up miles of barbed wire and barricaded the train stations.

By 5 a.m., they had closed the border so that no one could cross over into East Berlin. Most importantly, none of the people living in East Berlin could go to West Berlin.

Armed guards were stationed all along the 97-mile border with orders to shoot people who tried to leave East Germany. In a few weeks, a concrete wall was built a few feet in front of the barbed wire. And in the countryside, chain-link fences and walls were installed along the entire length of East Germany's border with West Germany. Guard towers were erected with armed sentries watching 24 hours a day. And the area was filled with land mines and booby traps to discourage people from trying to escape.

The Communist Party believed Operation Rose was necessary to save its government. The people who lived in West Germany had a government that allowed them to vote for their political leaders. The people could own their own businesses and homes, and they had become a relatively prosperous nation with lots of personal freedom.

East Germans were not allowed to own their own businesses; the government ran all of the factories and shops. There were no free elections. The government even decided what jobs people would have. Many people in East Germany disliked the communist rule and had left East Germany to make their home in West Germany. In the 1950s, nearly 2.5 million people had emigrated from East Germany to West Germany and other democratic republics. East Germany was losing its population at an alarming rate. The communist leaders decided the way to stop it was to end all emigration and travel. The final stage was to build a wall through the city of Berlin. It was the last escape point out of East Germany.

When the people of Berlin woke up on Sunday morning, they were shocked. How could this have happened? And why didn't the United States or Great Britain or France come and tear down the wall?

Could You Climb the Wall?

The Berlin Wall was made of reinforced concrete and stood 12 feet high and almost 4 feet wide. The top of the wall was lined with a smooth pipe to make it harder to climb. It was reinforced with barbed wire, 116 watchtowers, guard dogs, and 24-hour armed guards. It stood until November 9, 1989, when East Germany announced that its citizens were free to visit West Germany.

Great Britain, the United States, and France hated the building of the wall, but the agreement had been made that the Soviet Union would rule over this part of Germany. The countries were afraid that if they went back on the agreement they had made at the end of World War II, it could start another war. And they knew that the Soviet Union could protect East Germany because it had already demonstrated its atomic bomb.

The United States, Great Britain, and France held to their agreement and allowed the Soviet Union to help East Germany build the wall. It stopped a war, but it left millions of people trapped in a communist country where they did not want to live. And it divided Berlin into two separate cities.

Families were divided. Grandparents who lived in West Berlin could not see grandchildren in East Berlin. Many East Berliners had attended college in West Berlin. They could not go to school or see their friends. Husbands were separated from wives and children. The communist government refused to allow anyone to leave East Berlin without special permission. And special permission was never granted to anyone who was suspected of wanting to leave permanently.

The East German government set up a special group of spies called the Stasi whose job was to find out about anyone who might want to leave East Germany. People who planned to escape were turned in by Stasi spies and sent to prison.

For 2 years, nobody could visit East Berlin without a special passport, but in 1963, people were granted permission to visit relatives on day trips for Christmas holidays. It wasn't until 1973 that West Germans and citizens of other countries were allowed to go to visit East Germany on a more regular basis. Then they could travel to visit family and friends if they were approved for a visa. Sometimes they could take a day trip into East Germany to visit their relatives, but the guards at the border could also refuse to allow people to enter East Germany at any time. They did not have to give a reason.

Because of the lack of freedom in East Berlin, many people wanted to leave. They suffered from harsh living conditions with limited quantities of food and basic necessities. They were given work quotas that were impossible to meet and then were not paid. A bad situation became intolerable, and they were desperate to escape.

They tried everything—from digging under the wall to flying over it. Some hid in the trunks of cars, and others packed themselves in crates and suitcases. It is estimated that 40,000 people made direct escapes from East Berlin to West Berlin. Thousands escaped with forged passports through other countries. But millions more were trapped for 28 years behind the Berlin Wall.

Venona-Style Codes

You can make your own super-secret, hard-to-crack code just like the Soviets did. All you need is paper, pencil, some time, and your super sneaky spy brain.

The Venona Code used number substitutions for letters and words. The thing that made it special is that the spies were never supposed to use the same code twice. This makes it tough, because every time you want to send a secret message you have to have another code. But it makes it super hard for your enemies to decipher.

You can use this code as a starting point. Make simple words that you use often into a number.

For example:

the - 1	and - 2	meet - 3	spy - 4
package - 5	run - 6	time - 7	enemy - 8
target - 9	code - 10	night - 11	day - 12

Then assign random numbers to the rest of the alphabet.

A-52	B-97	C-63	D-100	E-41	F-33
G-21	H-19	I-77	J-23	K-65	L-29
M-34	N-45	O-13	P-15	Q-91	R-85
S-53	T-76	U-102	V-42	W-60	X-101
Y-99	Z-54				

Practice by cracking this code:
33 77 45 100 1 5 2 6 1 8 4 19 52 53 63 52 102 21
19 76 99 13 102

Now try creating your own code to share with a friend. Just remember that to keep it totally secure you need to make a new code for every message!

Answer: *Find the package and run. The enemy spy has caught you.*

SPY TRAINING

Rocket Launch

You can become a rocket launch expert by building your own launch pad.

Materials:

- ❏ Large disposable plastic cups
- ❏ At least two rubber bands
- ❏ Scissors
- ❏ Masking or duct tape

First cut your rubber bands so they lay flat and make a knot on each end. Then cut four one-inch slits in the rim of the plastic cup. The slits should be opposite each other. (You might want to ask an adult to help with the cutting because it gets a little tricky.) Make sure the slits are no longer than one inch. You can reinforce the slits with the tape to prevent the cup from splitting apart.

Then slip the rubber bands into the slits so that they form a cross in the middle of the cup. This is your rocket. Use the other cup as the launch pad. You can decorate it or just leave it plain.

To launch the rocket, set the ordinary cup on the ground, mouth down. Then place the rubber band rocket cup on top, mouth down, like you are stacking them. Push firmly on the cup so that you feel the rubber bands stretching, then let go! Your rocket will fly!

TOP SECRET

East German tomb of the unknown soldier

A GDR Border Guard fleeing across the barbed wire to West Berlin, 1961

The Cambridge Spies

Kim Philby

Guy Burgess

Donald Maclean

The spy was quiet as he closed the door of his apartment. He cautiously looked around to see if anyone was watching him, but no one was paying attention. It was a stormy January night in 1963, and everyone was huddled inside away from the pounding rain.

The rain was excellent cover for the spy. Few people would be out on such a stormy night. It would be easy to see if anyone was following him. The spy made his way through the streets of Beirut, Lebanon, down to the port, where there was a ship waiting for him. The spy was relieved when the ship finally set sail. He had managed to escape. He would not be caught or stand trial in England and now he would spend the rest of his life in communist Russia.

The next few weeks, the newspapers in both Britain and the United States were full of the story. Kim Philby, a man who had worked for both the British Spy Agency MI6 and the

American CIA had defected to the Soviet Union. For nearly 25 years, Kim Philby had worked as a spy for the KGB, giving away U.S. and British military secrets to the Soviets and causing damage to numerous secret operations. Both nations were outraged.

Even more frustrating was the fact that 9 years prior, Philby had been under suspicion of being a spy, but the British Foreign Secretary had stood up in the House of Commons and defended him. Philby had been cleared of suspicion and later allowed to return to work for the MI6. Philby was the lead spy in what became known as the Cambridge Spy Ring— one of the greatest acts of treason in British history.

When Philby was a student at Cambridge, he was interested in communist politics. He liked the communist motto "From each, according to his ability, to each according to his need." He believed that the world would be a better place if the government owned businesses and equally divided the wealth among its citizens. He joined the student-led communist organization at Cambridge and through this group, he met other young people who also believed in communism.

Two of his friends were Donald Maclean and Guy Burgess. All three of the young men were born into rich and privileged families. Their families had friends who were high officials in the British government and military. They were just the type of people the KGB wanted to recruit.

Philby was the first to agree to act as a spy for the Soviet Union. He thought he could further the cause of communism by giving information to the Soviet Union. He was assigned a handler, a Soviet spy who was his boss. He was also given the code name Stanley. Then he was asked if he could suggest other Cambridge students who might also be willing to become KGB spies. Maclean and Burgess were happy to join their friend in the spy business.

All through WWII, the men appeared to be working for the British. But they were secretly sending reports back to the

Soviet Union. Maclean sent a 60-page report about the uranium bomb to the KGB. Burgess worked for the British foreign minister and transmitted top-secret documents directly to the KGB. And Philby was so good at pretending to be a loyal British subject that he was assigned to be the British head of counter espionage. All the while, Philby was feeding information directly to the Soviet Union.

Their covers began to unravel because of the code breakers working on Venona. The American cryptographers were able to uncover the code name Homer and found that Homer had given bomb secrets to the Soviets.

In 1951, Philby learned that his friend, Maclean was going to be exposed as a spy. He knew that if Maclean was caught, it could mean execution for all of them. So he made a plan with Burgess to warn Maclean and get him out of the country. Burgess would then silently return to England, and they would say they knew nothing about Maclean's disappearance.

Tinker, Tailor, Soldier, Spy

John Le Carré

Several books and movies have been written based on the Cambridge spies and their work. One of the most famous is *Tinker, Tailor, Soldier, Spy.* It was written by John Le Carré, a former spy himself. He worked for MI6 and MI5 in the 1950s and 1960s and was one of the spies betrayed by Kim Philby.

It didn't quite work out that way. Burgess decided to defect to the Soviet Union with Maclean rather than run the risk of being caught as a spy in England. The defection of two prominent government officials to the Soviet Union made headlines around the world. British agents were furious. Who had tipped them off so they could escape?

Immediately people began accusing Philby of being a spy, too. He adamantly denied the accusations and an investigation could turn up no real proof of his spying. Prominent people like the British foreign secretary defended him and Philby was fired from his job at British Intelligence MI6. But without any hard evidence, Philby was never prosecuted and eventually even hired back by the MI6.

For 9 more years, Philby kept on spying, sending information to the KGB. He supplied names of British agents to the KGB and many of them were captured and executed. He also gave information about military plans that helped the KGB in their fight against England and America.

But on January 10, 1963, Philby was confronted by an old friend, Nicholas Elliot. Elliot offered Philby immunity if he would confess and give the British information on the KGB. Philby agreed, but secretly he contacted the KGB and arranged for his own escape.

After the defection of Philby, the British government was horribly embarrassed and afraid of more spies. They discovered at least two more men who had been students at Cambridge who were also acting as spies.

Experts agree that the Cambridge spies were some of the most successful KGB informants, and it is difficult to calculate the number of agents who were killed because of the Cambridge spies' betrayal. It could number in the hundreds.

Philby, Maclean, and Burgess spent the rest of their lives in the Soviet Union living under the communist regime they served.

Clever Girl

Elizabeth Bentley

Her code name was Clever Girl, and Elizabeth Bentley was certainly smart. She graduated from Vassar College in the 1930s when many women never attended college. She traveled the world and learned to speak Italian and French and attended graduate school at Columbia University.

It was while she was studying at Columbia University that she became interested in the communist government and joined the Communist Party of the United States. She believed in the cause of communism and thought that a communist world would be a better civilization. She vowed she would do anything she could to help the communist cause.

Elizabeth sought out and received a job as a librarian at the Italian Library of Information in New York City. The library was actually used by the Italian government to promote their fascist or dictator-style regime—a government that the Communist Party despised. Elizabeth knew this and wanted to use her new job to help the Communist Party. She offered to become a spy.

Elizabeth's handler was Jacob Golos. Jacob had emigrated from Russia to the United States and had become a U.S. citizen. He taught Elizabeth the tricks of the spy trade, like how to steal documents and pass information to other spies. Elizabeth was quick to learn and soon she was not only collecting information, but also helping to recruit additional spies.

Jacob then recruited Elizabeth to expand her work to spy for the Soviet Communist Party. She agreed, and soon she was in charge of a large group of spies trading information back and forth across the globe.

Throughout World War II, Elizabeth believed she was helping the brave Russians beat the Nazi war machine with her information. The Soviets considered her an important spy in their network.

But at the end of the war, Elizabeth began to realize that the Soviet Union was not going to enact a communist government the way Elizabeth had envisioned. She realized that many of the government leaders were interested in their own welfare and self-promotion. She felt betrayed.

Elizabeth decided to go to the FBI with her information. She would ask for protection from prosecution in exchange for the information she could give. She thought that perhaps this information would stop some of the Soviet leaders and perhaps she could still help her communist cause.

The FBI was thrilled to receive Elizabeth's information. She was able to name close to 150 people who were spying for the Soviet Union. The FBI hoped they would be able to use Elizabeth as a double agent, but Kim Philby, another undercover KGB agent, reported her to the Soviet Union. She went from being the KGB's clever girl to a traitor and a woman wanted by the KGB.

Elizabeth never did return to spying. She worked as a secretary and a teacher. She also gave lectures on the communist threat. She died from cancer in 1963 at the age of 55.

Spy Disaster

It seemed like a normal day to Robert Schaller. In 1965, he was a young doctor doing his rounds at the University of Washington Hospital when he heard his name on the intercom. When he got to the lobby, Robert was met by a man who looked like a spy, complete with dark glasses and a tan trench coat. Robert wondered what was going on.

> "How would you like to go to the Himalayas?" The man asked.

Robert was stunned. As an avid mountain climber, the Himalayas were his dream. But how did this man know that? And who was he?

The man showed his credentials and explained that he was from the CIA and they were looking for someone to help them with a secret mission. They needed someone who had experience in extreme mountain climbing and a medical background. The CIA knew that Robert had just returned from a trip to Alaska to climb Denali. They also knew he had been a college athlete. Now the CIA wanted to know if Robert was willing to serve his country as a spy on a very top secret mission that involved climbing the Himalayan Mountains. Robert Schaller said yes.

> He was taught how to detonate explosives, how to jump out of a helicopters, and how to handle nuclear equipment.

His training began immediately. Robert's employers at the hospital were given the cover story that Robert was training to be a physician astronaut. The hospital granted him leave for his training missions, but Robert could never tell what he was actually doing or where he was going.

Most of the time, Robert didn't know where he was going. He would be picked up in a car and blindfolded. He then had to crawl through a canvas tunnel to reach the airplane and the windows of the plane were blacked out so he would not know where he had been flown.

Robert had to learn to do the work of a spy. He was taught how to detonate explosives, how to jump out of a helicopters, and how to handle nuclear equipment. Then Robert was told the true nature of their mission.

One year earlier, the United States had detected a nuclear test blast in China. The U.S. government was shocked because it had not known that China had the scientific capabilities to build a nuclear bomb. But atmospheric tests done by scientists in India had confirmed that there had been nuclear activity in China. Both the governments of America and India were gravely concerned. They teamed up to figure out a way to spy on China's nuclear weapons development.

The photos in spy satellites would not give the information they needed and the Chinese could detect high-flying spy planes. They needed to put surveillance in place where China would never detect it. The Indian government offered the perfect spot, Nanda Devi, one of the tallest mountains in the Himalayan range.

A plan began to take shape. The Americans would construct a powerful electronic eye and with the help of India's famous mountain climbing guides, scientists would install the device on the mountain overlooking China.

Robert was one of the small team of mountain climbing scientists who would scale the massive mountain and put the electronic eye in place. It would be a dangerous climb. Only six people had ever reached the 25,000-foot summit of Nanda Devi and three of them had died before they returned to the ground. Robert and the other scientists would not just be climbing, but would also be carrying a 40-pound plutonium-powered generator along with all of the other equipment.

In the fall of 1965, the team was prepared to make their ascent. Local guides called Sherpa had been hired to help the team make the climb. Together there were about a dozen climbers ready to scale Nanda Devi.

Robert said he was excited about the climb. He felt like he was doing something to help protect his nation from a nuclear attack, and he was thrilled to be in the Himalayas. It was a climber's dream.

For several days, the team made their way up the mountain. The generator with its plutonium 238 and 239 cells glowed with heat and the Sherpa would snuggle up to it at night. Robert tried not to think about the radioactivity of the generator. He knew that with the nuclear power the electronic eye would keep working for decades and would ensure that America and India could see China's activities.

The climb went well. Scientists used steel-spiked shoes and ice axes to help them cross the icy glaciers, and Robert recorded details of the trip in his journal and with his camera. At last, they reached High Camp. The summit of the mountains was just 1,000 feet above them. It was there that disaster struck.

A blizzard blew onto the mountain. If the team did not go back down they would die in the cold and ice. But what were they going to do about all of the equipment they had just hauled up the mountain? Could they make it down the mountain with all of the heavy equipment? Would it be safe to leave the equipment there? The expedition leader, Captain Kohli, made the decision to tie down the equipment and leave

Corkscrew Tanks

The Soviets tried to prepare for every type of warfare, including fighting on glaciers and snow. They built a corkscrew tank that moved on giant—well—corkscrews. It worked well in moving through snow and ice but was not very fast. They discovered they could modify the design to make a corkscrew-powered boat. They used an amphibious corkscrew vehicle called the ZIL-2906 to rescue cosmonauts who landed in inaccessible areas.

it on the mountain. They would return in the spring and haul it the rest of the way up to the summit.

Robert was opposed to this idea. He didn't think it was a good idea to leave a nuclear generator on the mountain for several months, but he was overruled. The generator and all of the other parts were lashed together and left on Nanda Devi as the team made its escape from the storm.

In the spring, Robert returned with the team and climbed back up the mountain. They reached High Camp and looked for the crag where they had left their equipment, but it was gone. As a matter of fact, an entire shelf of the mountain was gone, sheared off in an avalanche. The nuclear generator was nowhere to be found.

This presented an alarming problem. If the nuclear generator was buried under the moving ice of the glacier, the plutonium could eventually be ground down and end up in ice melt. It could flow down to rivers and contaminate drinking water for thousands of people.

> If the nuclear generator was buried under the moving ice of the glacier, the plutonium could eventually be ground down and end up in ice melt.

The CIA sent a cleanup team to see if they could locate the nuclear generator. They searched for 2 years, but were never able to locate the missing equipment.

Robert and his team were assigned a new mountain peak and outfitted with another electronic eye. This time the climb was a success, and the spy device was installed. But the CIA required one more thing from Robert—his notebooks and pictures. The CIA confiscated all of his records of the climbs and never returned them.

Robert returned to his work as a doctor and did not talk about his work for the CIA until 40 years later when his part in the project was revealed in a book by the expedition leader, Captain Kohli.

The Scholar Spy

The KGB thought they had found the right man for the job. Boris Yuzhin was sent to the University of California at Berkeley in the summer of 1975. He already had a postgraduate degree, so his cover story was that he was a visiting academic in the U.S. to do research. In reality, he was supposed to be scouting for Berkeley students who might be willing to become spies for the KGB.

But instead of Boris convincing American students to become loyal to the Soviet government, Boris became loyal to America. He said within a week of arriving in America, he felt he could finally breathe. He could talk openly with students about what they liked and disliked in the United States. And the American students asked him lots of questions. Questions he couldn't answer.

The American students wanted to know what was happening with the political prisoners in the Soviet Union. Boris said he was ashamed to admit he knew very little about the people who had been imprisoned for their political or religious views. He wanted to argue with the Americans that they were wrong about his government, but he didn't know the facts. Information like that was not published in Soviet newspapers or broadcast on the evening news.

So Boris started doing some research of his own. He spent his days in the library reading Soviet authors whose books were banned by the KGB. He did research about the political prisoners and the people who had vanished after they had a disagreement with the KGB. Soon he realized that he had been deceived. The country that promised to treat every worker the same actually treated the workers badly and rewarded the politicians with great wealth. Boris was angry with the Soviet government for lying to its own citizens. He knew he had to do something to help. He decided to offer his services to the United States as a spy.

> Boris was angry with the Soviet government for lying to its own citizens. He knew he had to do something to help. He decided to offer his services to the United States as a spy.

The United States gladly accepted, and for the next several months, Boris taught FBI agents about the methods the Soviet officers used to obtain information. He informed them of spies who had infiltrated the U.S. government and showed them where there were information drops.

After 10 months, Boris had to return to the Soviet Union. His work as a U.S. spy was not discovered, and 2 years later, the KGB sent him back to San Francisco. This time, he was posing as a reporter for the Soviet news agency TASS. He immediately returned to his work as a spy for America.

The FBI was thoroughly impressed with Boris and his spy abilities. His handlers considered him a "rock star" because of the amazing amount of information he was able to get for America. One time, he even managed to photocopy the annual report of the KGB political branch. He helped uncover an espionage ring in Norway and gave almost daily information on different projects of the KGB.

His handlers think that part of why Boris was so successful is that he didn't look or act at all like the stereotypical spy.

The Big Dog Escape

Would you believe one secret agent made his escape disguised as a dog? During the 1970s, the CIA came up with a plan to get one of its operatives out of Europe disguised as a St. Bernard. The operative wore a fake dog suit and was concealed in a large dog kennel. Nobody was suspicious when the dog was taken to the veterinarian for a check-up and the operative made his escape.

He was not tall and dashing. He was rather short and portly. He looked like a quiet professor. He looked ordinary and for-gettable. He could blend in with any crowd and people would not remember him. He was also quiet and soft-spoken, never calling attention to himself. For many years, he was able to work as a double agent without anyone suspecting the scholar was a spy.

But in December of 1986, everything changed. Boris, who was back in Moscow, was summoned by his Soviet chief. There he was told he had been named as a spy, and they began a harsh interrogation. But Boris realized that the KGB didn't have all of the information. They were hoping to learn more by intimidating him. So Boris began telling half-truths that would not hurt his American counterparts. He also told the KGB that the FBI was a terrible organization that had exploited him and forced him to work for them. The KGB authorities were happy to believe the story. Boris was tried and convicted of being a spy for America, but unlike many spies, he was not sentenced to death. He was given 15 years in a Siberian prison.

His time in the prison camp was one of grueling work and physical torture. He was not given much food and was beaten. But Boris never regretted his decision to spy for America. He said that his imprisonment confirmed his belief of how unfair the communist system was.

"The more I thought, the more I realized I did the right thing," he said, "because I got another taste of the system."

After 5 horrible years, Boris was released because the Soviet Union's government began to fall apart. Boris likes to think he was a small part of the reason the great Soviet com-munist experiment failed.

Today, Boris lives in California with his wife, Nadia. He is retired but sometimes lectures about the Soviet Union and communism. He also does research for the Ark Project helping to find information about missing Soviet political prisoners.

Grandma Was a Spy

Melita Norwood loved gardening and making jam. She looked just like any other grey-haired granny in Britain, but in 2005, the world found out that the 87-year-old grandma had been a KGB spy for 40 years. And not just any spy: The Soviet Union considered her one the most valuable spies in its agency.

Her code name was Hola and her KGB handler described her as a "loyal, trustworthy, disciplined agent." Melita did not do her spy work for any financial reward. Her parents had been strong supporters of the Communist Party, and Melita firmly believed in the principles of communism. She felt that the best way she could help the communist cause was to become a spy.

Melita didn't do her spy work with a gun and a trench coat. Her weapons were a typewriter and a secretarial job. In 1932, Melita took a job as a clerk at a company named the British Non-Ferrous Metals Research Association. She never mentioned to her boss that she was a member of the Communist Party and he never asked.

The company was actually involved in nuclear research, and Melita knew that the information would be highly valuable to the communists in the Soviet Union. Melita was a hard worker and earned the trust of both her boss at the company and her handler at the KGB. Her job was to take the files from her boss's safe, photograph them, and then deliver them to the KGB.

Ethel Rosenberg

Not all spies got off as easily as Melita Norwood. **Ethel Rosenberg** and her husband were convicted of giving the Soviet Union plans for how to make an atom bomb. As U.S. citizens, this was considered high treason. They were given the death sentence and executed in 1953.

All through WWII and on into the Cold War, Melita kept the documents flowing to the KGB. She was promoted in the company and was given a top security clearance, which allowed her access to more important papers and plans.

She married Hillary Norwood, a fellow communist. She had a daughter and lived in a quiet British neighborhood. And all the while, she kept up her work as a spy for the KGB.

She retired from the company and her spy work at the same time. She had spent nearly 40 years as the quiet reliable secretary who also happened to be a spy. She was never caught.

But in 1999, top-secret KGB documents were uncovered and the identity of Hola the spy was revealed. By this time, Melita was 87 years old and living in a retirement community. Nobody could believe that the sweet little old lady had been a KGB agent. Even her daughter was shocked.

> Melita didn't do her spy work with a gun and a trench coat. Her weapons were a typewriter and a secretarial job.

Melita admitted that yes, she had been spying for the Communist Party and that she had no regrets about it. She believed in the communist experiment and was prepared to go to prison or die for the cause. Neither was required of her. The British government decided that it would not be in its best interest to prosecute a little old lady for crimes that happened decades before.

Melita continued to garden, make jam, and talk to her neighbors about the value of communism until her death at the age of 93.

The Spy Who Skied

Peter Lunn loved the rush of adrenaline he felt as he bar-reled down the ski slopes. The faster he could go, the more he loved it. And falling was just a part of the excitement. If he didn't fall once in a while, then he believed he wasn't trying hard enough. And Peter was all about trying hard at every-thing he did.

Peter grew up on the slopes of Switzerland. His famous British grandfather, Sir Henry Lunn, was a great promoter of alpine downhill skiing as a sport and Peter's father was instru-mental in getting downhill skiing included in the Olympics. Peter himself represented Britain in the 1936 Winter

Olympics. He came in a disappointing 15th place, and later said he "skied too carefully."

When war broke out, Peter joined the Royal Artillery, but his supervisors soon realized that his real skills were not being used and he was moved to the Secret Intelligence Service (SIS). He was posted to both Malta and Italy, where he worked to uncover information that could help the Allies in the war against the Nazis. As a part of his spy training, he took a parachute course and later said that parachuting was an activity that provided "maximum fright with minimal risk."

After the war, Peter continued working for Britain's MI6 and was made the head of the Vienna station. It was the start of the Cold War, and Peter was aware that it was critical to get information on what the Soviet Union was planning. The U.S. and British generals desperately wanted to know if the Soviets were planning to use their nuclear weapons on the West. They needed a way to listen in on their conversations. Peter found a way.

> Peter began to investigate and learned that there were Soviet telephone cables running through the British and French sectors of Vienna. If he could tap into these cables without the Soviets knowing, then he would have access to Soviet communication.

Graham Greene, an old acquaintance from his days with the SIS, came to Vienna to do research for a screenplay he was writing. Graham began crawling through the tunnels beneath the city of Vienna and discovered something strange. There were people in the sewers who were guarding something. Graham reported this to Peter.

Peter began to investigate and learned that there were Soviet telephone cables running through the British and French sectors of Vienna. If he could tap into these cables

BRIDGE OF SPIES

During the Cold War, many spies were captured by enemy governments. The U.S. and the Soviet Union often made deals to get their spies back by making a prisoner exchange. Often they used the Glienicke Bridge as their exchange site. The bridge connected communist Germany with West Germany, so it was considered a neutral site. At least 40 spies were returned to their countries on the Glienicke Bridge.

without the Soviets knowing, then he would have access to Soviet communication.

Immediately Peter's team went into action. The first thing Peter did was purchase a house that sat directly over the lines of cables. Then, hidden away from Soviet eyes, Peter had his team from MI6 begin digging. He also recruited a private mining consultant who helped him construct three tunnels that were used to tap the Soviet phone lines. From 1948 until 1951, Peter's team could listen in on every conversation that went on in the Soviet headquarters in Vienna.

In 1953, Peter was promoted to be the MI6 station chief in Berlin. The tensions in Berlin were high with lots of conflict between the communist East Berlin and the more democratic West Berlin. Americans were still afraid that the Soviets would attack and American defense secretary George Marshall declared, "I don't care what it takes, all I want is 24 hours' notice of a Soviet attack."

Peter's suggestion was to use the wiretapping method that had been so successful in Vienna. Winston Churchill approved Peter's plan and digging began in Berlin. The project was code named Operation Gold and was a joint venture between the Americans and the British.

It took months of planning and digging, but in May of 1955, the wiretap was successfully placed. The first message sent to Washington, DC, was "The baby is born." For a year, MI6 operatives listened to all of the conversations flowing back and forth between East Berlin and the Soviet Union.

But in April of 1956, the Soviets declared that they had discovered the tunnel. Peter learned that one of his most trusted spies had actually been a double agent working for the KGB. That agent had told the Soviets all about Operation Gold. It was a huge disappointment for everyone involved, but the intelligence information that they had gained during that year was so vast that it took them until 1958 to finish processing it all.

During the 1960s, Peter was the MI6 chief in Beirut and continued to work to fight the Cold War with his spies and information gathering. And every chance he got, he would spend time on the slopes skiing.

Peter "retired" from his spy work in 1972, but was frequently called back by MI6 to consult on special projects, teach classes, and give lectures. He didn't talk much about his work as a spy, too much of it was top secret. But he was always willing to talk about skiing. He died in 2011 at the age of 97 and had kept skiing until he was 96.

The Magician Spy

John Mulholland stood in front of his audience. Women were dressed in fancy evening gowns, and men wore suits and ties. It was a small group of people at a very exclusive, very expensive dinner party. He asked a woman at the party to blindfold him. Once the lady had made sure the blindfold was secure and that there was no way he could see, he asked his assistant to go around the room with a tray and collect an item from each person. One man placed his eyeglasses on the tray, another put his wristwatch, and two ladies put rings. The assistant went to every person until the tray was full.

Then, with Mulholland still blindfolded at the front of the room, the assistant held up each object on the tray one at a time. Magically, Mulholland was able to identify every single item. Stunned, his audience dared him to do it again. He happily obliged and once again amazed the guests by getting every item right. They left for dinner still talking about the astonishing trick.

Mulholland smiled—it was one of his easier tricks and he had been well paid for a simple night's work. The next night he would be performing on stage in front of hundreds of people and the next week he would be lecturing on the history of magic. It was a busy life for one of the world's best magicians.

During the 1930s and 1940s, Mulholland dazzled crowds with his incredible stage tricks and mind reading. He began training as a magician in 1911 when he was just 13 years old. He started performing on stage when he was only 15. By the time he was in his 30s, he was a well-known magician, traveling the world performing and teaching magic tricks. He was so famous that he was invited by President Franklin Roosevelt to perform at the White House eight different times. Mulholland wrote 10 books on magic and illusion, traveled to 42 different countries, and was the editor of the magician's magazine, *The Sphinx*. But his most amazing job was one he performed in total secret.

In the early 1950s, the CIA contacted Mulholland to see if he would be interested in doing some work for the agency. Mulholland was intrigued. What did the United States spy agency need from a magician? They wanted to learn his tricks.

With the Cold War raging, American spies needed to know how to deliver messages and packages without being detected. The Soviet and German governments had been training spies for decades. Spy craft was relatively new to the United States and the leaders at the CIA believed that professional training in the art of illusion would help the American spies be more successful. They needed a teacher.

Mulholland accepted the job and began training special agents in the art of magic. Misdirection is one of the most important techniques that he taught. A magician will use a lovely woman as an assistant, not because he needs help with the magic but because she will distract the audience from what the magician is actually doing. Mulholland advised spies to do the same thing. They were to learn how to distract people from seeing what was actually happening. The spies should misdirect their "audience."

For example, a spy who knew he was being watched would take the same route to work every day. After weeks of watching the spy walk down the street, under the bridge, and through the park, the enemy would see his commute as routine. This would allow the spy to deliver packages and messages in the moments when he was "out of sight." When the spy was under the bridge or hidden by trees, he would drop his package and the enemies would never suspect because they didn't see anything unusual.

Mulholland also told the CIA how to use the tools of magicians. He explained how he could make a coin disappear by having it attached to an elastic band hidden in his coat sleeve. The CIA agent could hide and deliver weapons or packages in the same way.

Another trick was using "doubles" to help people escape or defect from the Soviet Union and East Berlin. The agent and the defector had to be of similar height and weight. Both would appear at a party or large gathering dressed in opposite-style clothes. At some point in time, they would change their costumes and the CIA agent would take the place of the defector at the party. Another agent would then escort the defector out of the country. By the time the KGB noticed the change, it was too late to find the defector. This is the same trick magicians use to make it appear that they have moved their assistant from one side of the stage to another. They use doubles—only they are dressed exactly alike. Mulholland showed the CIA that what works on stage also works for spies.

Another magician's trick is to use the clothes he is wearing to conceal special tools. Heels of shoes hid microfilm cartridges, and raincoats had secret pockets to hold weapons such as poison ink pens and lock-picking tools. If a spy was caught, he had a secret slit in one pocket that could be used to throw away incriminating evidence.

Mulholland's training efforts were considered quite successful, and the CIA had him write a top-secret manual for its spies. It was titled *Some Operational Applications of the Art of Deception and Recognition Signals.* Considered a highly classified document, the CIA wanted the agency protected in case the manual fell into the wrong hands, so there were no references to "agents or "operatives." Instead they were called "performers," and they were taught "tricks."

It is not known exactly how long Mulholland worked for the CIA. There is evidence that he helped develop some of the tools the spies used, such as cameras hidden in cigarette lighters and electronic listening devices. But John Mulholland went to his grave never telling anyone about the work he did as the CIA's magician. He died in 1970 at the age of 71. In 1973, all records of Mulholland's work and his manual were destroyed. For more than 30 years, there was no substantial proof that Mulholland had really served as a consultant to the CIA. But in 2007, a long lost copy of the manual was found and published under the name *The Official CIA Manual of Trickery and Deception.* Now a whole new generation can learn about Mulholland's tricks just by checking the book out of the library.

Animal Agents

What do a raven, a cat, and a dolphin have in common? They were all trained as agents for the CIA.

During the Cold War, advanced technologies were just being developed. Mini cameras and tiny recording devices were the latest and greatest technology. There were no lasers, no digital cameras, no cell phones, and no notebook computers. Robotics was the stuff of science fiction. Secret agents needed a way to get close to their targets without being detected, and animals seemed like the best bet.

Nobody pays attention to the stray cat that wanders the alley. Birds fly around buildings and land on window ledges all of the time. And dolphins are often seen next to boats in the ocean. No one would ever suspect that the animals were actually highly trained spies.

Military-type animal training started in WWII when famous psychologist B. F. Skinner trained pigeons to "drive" a missile to a designated target. Two of Skinner's students, Keller Breland and his wife, Marian, continued to research and teach animals after the end of the war. They started a business called Animal Behavior Enterprises and trained animals for use in movies and television.

They opened up the IQ Zoo in Hot Springs, AR, and invited the public to view their animals. Families were delighted to watch chickens play tic-tac-toe and raccoons dunk basketballs. The IQ Zoo was called upon to train animals for companies like Disney and General Mills. Soon the CIA came knocking at the door.

At the same time the Brelands were training animals at the IQ Zoo, Bob Bailey was working with the Navy to train dolphins and sea lions as secret operatives. The highly intelligent sea mammals were taught to detect sea mines and enemy swimmers.

Eventually Bailey joined the Brelands at the IQ Zoo. Together they worked on several projects for the CIA, including how to train cats and ravens to act as spies.

Bomb Bees

Scientists are still researching ways that animals can help the military. Researchers at DARPA (Defense Advanced Research Laboratory) have discovered that they can train honeybees to smell explosives. A swarm of honeybees would not be welcome in an airport, but could be a great tool in a war zone.

View the Zoo
You can watch a video of the IQ Zoo at
http://www.youtube.com/watch?v=Egm_98WbE4s.

Acoustic Kitty was a project that the CIA hoped to use to listen to enemy conversations. The plan was to implant listening devices under the skin of a cat and teach the cat to wander in and out of spaces where enemy agents were known to meet. It is unclear whether this plan was ever actually put into play, because all of the documents are still classified. What is known is that the people at the IQ Zoo admit that they worked on training cats to carry out some specific tasks and they verify that the cats were successful in their learning.

Ravens were also on the CIA agent list. Ravens are large birds that are able to carry significant weight in their beaks and still fly. The plan was to embed a listening device into an object and have the raven place it on a window ledge of an enemy office. The device could be hidden in a piece of concrete so that it looked like a chip off of a building, or it could be hidden in a fake acorn or nut. Anything that would look natural on a window ledge. Ravens were also coached to pick up items from a room and carry them out the window.

Again, there is no official verification that ravens were used in this way because all of the documents are still considered top secret and are not released to the public.

One report that *is* open to the public is the training of pigeons as spies of enemy attack. Pigeons learned to fly with Army troops. If the pigeons detected that an enemy unit was advancing or ready to give a surprise attack, the pigeons would land and the army would have advance warning of the attack. This worked well if there was an enemy ready to attack, but if there was no enemy, the pigeons never landed and just kept flying. The program was cancelled because they lost too many trained pigeons.

Ski Team Race

Spies work as a part of a team. They depend on each other to send messages and share information. You can practice your spy teamwork and be on a ski team just like Peter Lunn.

Materials:

- ❏ Four yardsticks
- ❏ Four jump ropes
- ❏ Three friends

This activity will test your teamwork skills. The objective is to see which team can "ski" the fastest. Divide into two teams of two. Give each team two yardsticks and two jump ropes. Lay the jump ropes on the ground and place the yardsticks perpendicular on top of the ropes.

Stand on the yardsticks like they are skis. Place one team member in front, and one in back. Use the jump ropes like ski poles. They will also help you hold the skis on your feet. It's tricky, but it can be done. Practice a bit before you race. The team that crosses the finish line first is the one with super teamwork skills!

SPY TRAINING

Parachute Men

Spies have to be able to parachute into dangerous territory and they learn to do so as part of their training. You can make a parachute with some simple materials.

Materials:

- ❏ A pen
- ❏ A plastic bag or plastic material
- ❏ Scissors
- ❏ String
- ❏ A small action figure (LEGO men work great!)

Draw an octagon shape onto your plastic bag. (An octagon has eight sides of equal length.) Cut a small hole near the corner of each side. This will be where you tie the parachute strings. Cut eight strings of equal length and tie one in each hole on the bag. Knot the other end of the eight strings together. Use another piece of sting to tie the knot to your action figure. He should now be ready for parachute training.

Get permission from an adult to launch your parachute from a deck or tall spot. See how it flies!

Special Missions

Urban combat training in Berlin

Company platoon and squad leaders receiving an Operations Order during a field exercise

Tunnels to Freedom

They started in the basement of an abandoned bakery. With picks and shovels, a group of college students broke through the basement floor and began digging in the sandy Berlin soil. It was a team of 30 young volunteers. A few of them knew each other, many didn't, but all of them knew the organizers. They introduced themselves by their first names and some of them used aliases. They didn't want to know too much about each other, so that if they were caught and tortured they wouldn't have any information to give.

Their mission was to dig a tunnel from the basement of the West Berlin bakery to the other side of the wall. They had to dig 50 feet under the Berlin Wall and make the tunnel 500 feet long so that it would open up in the bathroom of an old apartment building in East Berlin. The digging took months. To avoid making the East German border police suspicious, the volunteers divided into teams, and each team took turns living in the basement while digging. They only came out when it was time to change teams.

One of the diggers was Joachim Neumann. He had escaped from East Berlin right after the wall had gone up by using a fake pass- port. He vowed he would help other people get out of East Berlin includ- ing his girlfriend, Christa. He had already helped build a previous tunnel

> They had to dig 50 feet under the Berlin Wall and make the tunnel 500 feet long so that it would open up in the bathroom of an old apartment building in East Berlin.

under the wall. That tunnel had allowed 29 people to crawl to freedom before it flooded from a burst water pipe. But his girlfriend had been out of town and couldn't get back before the tunnel collapsed.

Joachim had worked on a second tunnel, and this time, Christa made her way into the tunnel only to be arrested for trying to leave the country. She was sentenced to 2 years in prison.

This was the third tunnel Joachim had worked on. He hoped Christa would be released from prison in time to try another escape, but he couldn't know for sure. He had tried to send messages to her through some of the runners, but he had not heard anything back. He kept digging. Even if he couldn't free Christa, at least he could help some other people find their way to freedom.

In East Berlin, Hans-Joachim Tillemann was waiting for a secret phone call. He had just been released from the hospital from emergency appendix surgery. His side was still sore and he had stiches, but when the phone call came, he was ready to go. He left the house and went to the address he had been given, Streiltzer Strasse 55. Inside the apartment building was a young man. Tillemann whispered the code word, "Tokyo."

> In East Berlin, Hans-Joachim Tillemann was waiting for a secret phone call. He had just been released from the hospital from emergency appendix surgery.

The man led Tillemann to an outdoor bathroom. There was a hole in the floor just large enough for a man to crawl into. Tillemann lowered himself into the tiny tunnel. Only 2 feet high and 3 feet wide, it had just enough space for him to crawl. Tillemann scrambled forward. He knew that if he was caught, he would either be imprisoned or killed. But if he wasn't caught, freedom waited at the end of the tunnel.

Tillemann wasn't the only person in the tunnel. He knew there were at least three other people crawling in front of him. Soon there was someone crawling behind him. They were all silent. The only noise was the sound of their breathing and the scratch of their hands and knees in the dirt.

Tillemann had no idea how long he had been crawling, but finally he reached the opening of the tunnel. Hands reached down to help him climb out. There was no victory cheer. The diggers still had to remain silent. But Tillemann was greeted by smiles and handshakes. He had made it to freedom.

Back in the bathroom, Joachim was waiting for the next group of escapees. He stood ready at the door listening for the code word. When a young woman said, "Tokyo," Joachim found himself staring at his girlfriend, Christa. She had just been released from prison and had received his message. She was ready to try to escape again. Joachim helped her climb into the hole and hoped she would make it to the other side.

That night both Tillemann and Christa made it safely to the freedom of West Berlin, as did many other East Berliners. But the next night was a disaster. The Stasi police and German troopers discovered the tunnel and raided it while people were still crawling through. The troopers pointed machine guns at the volunteers who were guarding the bathroom entrance. One of the volunteers, Christian Zobel, pulled out his handgun and fired. He was sure he had hit one of the police. Then the two volunteers dove into the tunnel and frantically crawled to the other side. Behind them they heard machine guns firing.

The tunnel was officially closed, but in those two nights, 57 people had managed to crawl under the wall and make an escape to freedom.

It was later reported that one of the East German troopers had been killed by the volunteers. Christian Zobel felt guilty his whole life believing he had killed the trooper. But after the fall of the Berlin Wall, it was revealed that the trooper had actually been killed by the machine gun fire from his own comrades. The Stasi had covered up that information to make the volunteer diggers look bad.

> The tunnel was officially closed, but in those two nights, 57 people had managed to crawl under the wall and make an escape to freedom.

Tillemann became a successful businessman in the West, and Christa and Joachim were happily married until her death 40 years later. It was a dangerous and daring plan for escape, but for 57 people, it was their best chance at freedom.

Operation Blue Peacock

TOP SECRET

It weighed 16,000 pounds and was codenamed the Blue Peacock. In 1957, this was Britain's first nuclear land mine. The government planned to place the mines in the plains of Germany with the intent of setting off the bombs if the Soviets began an invasion. The gigantic mines would be buried in the ground and could be detonated from a command post 3 miles away.

The problem was that the nuclear warhead had to be kept within a specific temperature range or the electronic parts of the bomb would stop working. Scientists were afraid that if they buried the bomb in the ground in Germany it would get too cold in the winter and the bomb would be useless.

The problem was that the nuclear warhead had to be kept within a specific temperature range or the electronic parts of the bomb would stop working.

Scientists came up with some unique ideas for how to keep the components warm. One proposal involved keeping live chickens in the bomb because their body heat would keep the electrical components warm. It was suggested that the chickens could be given enough food and water to let them remain alive through the cold snap. However there was no plan for how to safely dig up the mines and replace the chickens or how to keep the chickens from pecking on the wires.

Operation Blue Peacock was scrapped before it was actually deployed. Political leaders decided that the nuclear fallout was too dangerous and the giant bomb was never deployed.

The Story of
The Butter Battle Book

Dr. Seuss, the famous children's author, wrote a parable about the nuclear arms race called *The Butter Battle Book*. It told the story of a deadly war over the trivial idea of how to eat bread and butter. It was named a *New York Times* Notable Book of the Year in 1984, just 5 years before the end of the Cold War.

Last Train to Freedom

Harry Deterling was angry. Like many people in East Berlin, he resented the Communist Party and the wall they had put up. He didn't believe the East German leaders who kept telling everyone that the wall was there to protect them from aggression from the West. He knew the wall had been put up to keep people from leaving. To force them to live in a communist state. Harry was not going to stay.

Harry was a 27-year-old train engineer. His usual route once took him through the border into West Berlin, but now there were concrete barriers to block the trains from entering West Berlin. During the autumn, Harry made plans. He talked with the fireman on the train, his friend Hartmut Lichy. What if they tried something daring? Something unbelievable? What if they drove the train through the barricade and into West Berlin?

It was risky. They could be shot by East German border guards, or the train might not get through the barricade. If that happened, they would certainly be arrested for trying to escape. They could spend many years in a hard labor camp. But the two men thought it was worth the risk.

They set December 5 as their travel day, and very quietly, Harry and Hartmut talked to a few friends and family whom they could trust completely. They told them they were taking the "last train to freedom," and if they wanted to escape, then they needed to be on that train.

Harry drove the train like it was any ordinary day. People got on and off at different stations. Harmut did his usual work as the fireman. Nobody suspected a thing except for 24 special passengers, all friends and family who were riding the train to freedom.

At the Albrechtshof station, Harry was supposed to stop the train just in front of the new barricades. He had always stopped there before, but this time he didn't slow down at the station. He drove the train straight through the barricades and kept going. The border guards showered the train with bullets and all of the passengers ducked to the floor. Harry didn't stop the train until he reached the safety of Spandau, in West Berlin.

Harry and his friends piled off the train triumphant. They had made it to West Berlin. They would not be sent back by the sympathetic West Berliners.

Six other passengers and the conductor had no idea that they were going to be a part of a dramatic escape. The conductor and five of those passengers returned to their families

Over the Wall

Two daring young men escaped from East Berlin by making their own zip line. They shot an arrow from a five-story building to a shorter building just across the West Berlin Border. Attached to the arrow was a cable. Their friend attached the cable, and the two young men took a zip line ride over the dangerous area known as the death strip. Luckily, the German guard seemed to be taking a nap and they landed safely in the freedom of West Berlin.

in East Berlin. But one 17-year-old girl gladly stayed with the escape team. She had been separated from her family by the wall and had wanted to return to them.

It was an amazing ride to freedom—one that made headlines in newspapers around the world. The East German political leaders were angry. Escapes like this made them look bad. They became determined to stop anyone who wanted to leave East Germany. Border guards were ordered to shoot to kill. And they did just that. It is estimated that at least 125 people died trying to escape from East Berlin.

Project Iceworm

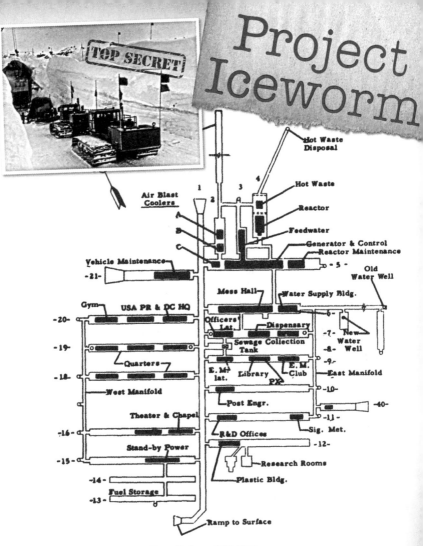

TOP SECRET

Hot Waste
Disposal

Air Blast
Coolers

1 3 4

2 A

Hot Waste

Reactor

Feedwater

Generator & Control

Reactor Maintenance

Vehicle Maintenance

-21-

- 5 -

Old
Water Well

Mess Hall

Water Supply Bldg.

Gym

USA PR & DC HQ

-20-

Officers'
Lat.

Dispensary

- 6 -

-19-

Sewage Collection
Tank

-7-

New
Water

-8-

Well

Quarters

E. M.
lat.

Library

E. M.
Club

-9-

East Manifold

PX

-18-

West Manifold

-10-

Theater & Chapel

Post Engr.

-40-

-16-

R&D Offices

-11-

Sig. Met.

Stand-by Power

-12-

-15-

Research Rooms

-14-

Plastic Bldg.

Fuel Storage

-13-

Ramp to Surface

Camp Century - Plan View

U.S. officials said it was a research outpost under the arctic ice of Greenland. They even made a movie about its construction. Camp Century was a small city buried under tons of ice and snow designed to let scientist and military experts learn how to work and survive in sub-zero temperatures. But in reality, it was a secret project known as Iceworm and it housed nuclear weapons that were aimed at the Soviet Union.

It began in 1959 with the construction of 21 ice trenches. The Army Corps of Engineers plowed out the deep trenches and covered the tops with corrugated metal roofs. The roofs were then covered with snow and ice, creating an underground city that housed 200 soldiers and scientists. It was just 800 miles from the North Pole and the average daily temperature was -10 degrees Fahrenheit. In the winter, the temperature could drop to -60 with winds over 100 mph. It was a hostile climate.

The military told the public all about the amazing technology that was being used to construct Camp Century. The artic camp was equipped with all of the modern conveniences like a library, theatre, chapel, and 10-bed hospital. They even had a hobby shop to keep the men busy on those long winter nights and a barbershop to keep them looking spiffy. The whole camp was powered by the world's first portable nuclear power plant with backup diesel generators just in case the nuclear power plant went down. It was considered an amazing feat of modern engineering, but it was a huge deception.

The real reason Camp Century was built was to house a new type of intercontinental ballistic missile called the Iceman. Greenland was strategically close to the Soviet Union. It gave the Americans and their allies an advantage in the event of a nuclear threat. The 600 Iceman missiles could be launched at a moment's notice and would be a great deterrent to the Soviets.

Unfortunately, the military didn't realize an important scientific fact: ice and glaciers move. At first the ice move-

OPERATION PAPERCLIP

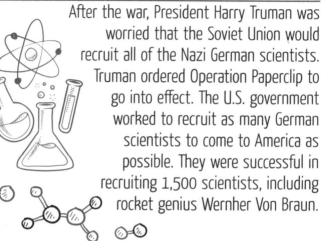

After the war, President Harry Truman was worried that the Soviet Union would recruit all of the Nazi German scientists. Truman ordered Operation Paperclip to go into effect. The U.S. government worked to recruit as many German scientists to come to America as possible. They were successful in recruiting 1,500 scientists, including rocket genius Wernher Von Braun.

ments were not very noticeable, some twisting of tunnels and movement of buildings. But after a few summers, the ice began to deform the tunnels and started to crush the buildings. In 1964, the army decided it was too unstable and removed the nuclear reactor and the missiles. Just 2 years later, the entire camp had to be closed. Within a few years, hundreds of sheets of ice had totally crushed and buried Camp Century.

> The ice core drillings that were taken during the construction of the camp are still used by scientists today to look at climate change . . .

There were some scientific discoveries that came from Camp Century. The ice core drillings that were taken during the construction of the camp are still used by scientists today to look at climate change and study environmental factors.

The Race for Space

TOP SECRET

Beep . . . beep . . . beep. In October of 1957, Americans huddled around their radios and listened to the noise. It was the sound of Sputnik, the first manmade satellite to be launched into space. It looked fairly harmless, like a silver beach ball with four antennae attached. But it terrified the world, because Sputnik was launched into space by the Soviet Union. If the Soviets could set a satellite into orbit around the Earth, surely they could launch bombs that could strike any-where in the world.

The Soviets were ecstatic and celebrated their scientific supremacy. They had done something that no other country had achieved, not even the mighty United States. The 183-pound satellite circled the Earth every 98 minutes; all the while, its radio beacon sent out the chilling beeping sound. The noise was proof to the public that Sputnik was real, and it caused fear and concern everywhere it was heard.

American newspapers warned that the United States was falling behind in the space race. The public urged increased math and science studies in schools and colleges. They wanted Congress to put more money into rocket development and scientific advancement. They wanted to get ahead of the Soviet Union.

It didn't get any better when just a month later the Soviets launched Sputnik 2. This time the satellite weighed 1,120 pounds and orbited the Earth for 200 days. It also carried a dog named Laika. The Soviets were the first country to launch

Inventions Race?

Besides getting man to the moon, the space race is credited with discoveries that led to many inventions we now use every day. Some of the inventions that can be directly linked to NASA are invisible braces, memory foam mattresses, the ear thermometer, athletic shoe insoles, scratch resistant eyeglasses, and adjustable smoke detectors. So the next time you visit the eye doctor or the dentist, you might want to thank an astronaut.

a living animal into space. Sadly, they never planned to have Laika return to Earth but just to study the effects of the animal while it was in space. Laika was the first dog to die in space.

The public outcry was huge. Americans were angry that the Soviets would experiment like that on a helpless dog. They were also worried about the Soviet domination of space. Why were the Soviets so far ahead? Could America ever catch up?

On December 6 of the same year, the U.S. Navy launched a rocket called Vanguard. But instead of showing the scientific accomplishments of America, it blew up on the launch pad in front of a national television audience. The U.S. military was humiliated. The Soviets had launched two successful satellites and the U.S. couldn't get its rocket off the launch pad. Newspapers ran headlines calling the failed satellite Flopnik, Kaputnik, and Dudnik. In a public meeting of the United Nations, the Russian delegate offered the U.S. representative aid "under the Soviet program of technical assistance to backwards nations."

American scientists quickly launched their next rocket, the Explorer 1, just a few weeks later on January 31, 1958. This launch was successful, and Americans finally had their own satellite circling the Earth.

Explorer 1 carried a cosmic ray detector and discovered the existence of radiation belts that circled the Earth. The satellite was 80 inches long and weighed about 30 pounds. It transmitted information back to Earth for more than 3 months. It was the success that the American public wanted. Now the United States was officially in the race to conquer space.

The leaders in Washington wanted to do everything they could to promote the new space program. On July 29, 1958, President Eisenhower signed the National Aeronautics and Space Act and created a new government agency called NASA. NASA's job was to give America the best space technology and to do it as fast as possible. It was critical that the

USS Flying Saucer?

In 1956, the U.S. Air Force experimented with building its own flying saucer. The plans called for a disc-shaped flying machine that would reach altitudes of 100,000 feet and fly at Mach 4. The machine they built didn't quite work as well as they hoped. It wobbled uncontrollably if it went any higher than 3 feet off the ground and its top speed was 35 mph. The project was scrapped.

United States be able to protect its people from possible space attacks by the Soviets. The U.S. had to win the space race.

But less than a year later, the Soviet space program took another leap forward when it launched the Luna Program. Luna 1 became the first spacecraft to orbit the sun, and Luna 2 was the first spacecraft to hit the moon. The closest any American probe had come to the moon at that point was 37,000 miles.

Then on October 4, 1959, the Soviet space program had its greatest triumph yet. It launched Luna 3. This spacecraft successfully orbited the moon and was able to photograph the dark side of the moon. No one had ever seen this before—it was an amazing feat of engineering. The world was awestruck. It seemed like the Soviet space program could do almost anything.

Then on April 12, 1961, the Soviet Union launched the first manned flight in space. Cosmonaut Yuri Gagarin blasted off on Vostok 1. He orbited the Earth for an amazing 108 minutes. As the spacecraft reentered Earth's atmosphere, Gagarin ejected from the ship and parachuted 23,000 feet to the Earth.

Meanwhile, the American scientists were frantically working on their own manned space flight. Just a month after Gagarin circled the Earth, the United States launched Mercury-Redstone 3. Astronaut Alan Shepard became the first American in space. During his 15-minute suborbital flight, he was able to observe the Earth from space and he ran tests on the space capsule's control system and retrorockets.

Shepard stayed inside the Mercury capsule for his re-entry. The capsule landed by parachute on the Atlantic Ocean near the Bahamas. A military helicopter picked up Shepard and his capsule.

America was catching up. But newly elected President John F. Kennedy didn't want America to be in second place. He was determined to win the space race. In May of 1961, he declared that the U.S. would land a man on the moon before the end of the decade. Americans were ecstatic. They felt like their government was working hard to protect them from the Soviet domination in space. Now it would be up to the scientists and engineers in America to see if they could beat the Soviet Union to the moon.

On May 25, 1961, President John F. Kennedy announced before a special joint session of Congress the goal of sending an American safely to the moon before the end of the decade

Operation Ivy Bells

USS *Halibut* preparing to fire a Regulus I missile, March 1960

The submarine silently slipped through the water. It moved slowly, searching for a cable on the bottom of the ocean floor. It was nearly an impossible task, especially hundreds of feet under the water in dark light and murky conditions. The submarine crew was supposed to find a cable that was only 5 inches in diameter. But it was such an important cable. If they found it, then they would hit the spy jackpot.

The submarine was the USS *Halibut* and it was on a special mission called Ivy Bells. Its job was to locate an underwater Soviet communication cable and tap it. The cable was located in Soviet waters and if the *Halibut* was caught, the Soviets would blow up the submarine. It was literally a life and death mission.

This mission was the brainchild of Captain James F. Bradley, who believed that if the U.S. could listen in on conversations between submarine bases and the Soviet leaders, it would learn invaluable secrets. The problem was to locate the cable. There weren't any signs pointing to a cable directly below. And the Soviets wanted to keep the cable secret. But

Captain Bradley had grown up near the Mississippi River, and he remembered that there were signs along the river that were only noticed by boat captains. Signs that warned the ships that communication cables were at the bottom of the river. He guessed that there would be similar signs warning Soviet submarine captains about the communication cable. He was right.

It took a week of searching, but his crew saw signs that warned of an underwater cable and narrowed down the area of where the cable could be found. As soon as they located the cable, they attached a special 3-foot long taping device to it. It contained a recorder filled with big rolls of tape. The tape would store a week's worth of conversations from the cable. Each week, a submarine crew would come back and pick up the tapes and put in new ones.

The project was a huge success. The Soviets did not think anyone could tap their conversations from an underwater cable, so they rarely encrypted their messages. The Navy was able to listen to information without having to crack a code. For more than 10 years, the Navy had an ear on everything that was going on with the Soviet submarine program. But in 1982, it became apparent that the Soviets had learned about the underwater tap.

In 1985, it was discovered that John A. Walker had betrayed the United States. The former Navy communication specialist had sold secrets to the Soviets, including the information about Operation Ivy Bells.

USS *Halibut* on the surface, full steam ahead, during sea trials, 1960

The Canadian Caper

The crowd of Iranian students outside the American Embassy grew louder and louder. They shouted protests against the United States government and burned the United States flag. For all of the American workers inside, it was a frightening time. Then it got worse.

On November 4, 1979, hundreds of Iranians stormed the embassy. They climbed over the walls, broke into the building and took the American workers hostage. It was a standoff that would last for 14 months before the hostages would be released.

Crowds of angry people filled the streets and anyone who was an American feared for his life. Most of the embassy employees were trapped inside, but six Americans managed to escape from the embassy compound.

Lee Schatz carefully walked through the angry mob. He kept his head down and didn't talk to anyone until he reached the Swedish Embassy. He took shelter inside the embassy and watched in fear as the angry crowd grew in numbers.

Five other Americans, Robert Anders, two of his staff members—Joe Stafford and Mark Liejek—and their wives managed to escape to Anders's apartment. They hid inside the small apartment and tried to figure out what to do. They knew that if the angry crowd found them, they would be arrested or, worse, tortured and killed. How were they going to escape and get to safety?

> They hid inside the small apartment and tried to figure out what to do. They knew that if the angry crowd found them, they would be arrested or, worse, tortured and killed.

Robert Anders called a friend of his at the Canadian Embassy and told him they were trapped in the apartment. Canadian ambassador Ken Taylor made arrangements for the group to be hidden in the Canadian Embassy. If anyone asked, they were to pretend to be Canadians working at the embassy. A few days later the Swedish ambassador called and asked if Lee Schatz could be hidden there as well.

The situation in Iran had not gotten any better. There were more than 50 Americans being held hostage at the former American Embassy, and there were riots going on across the city. If the Iranians found out that the Canadians were hiding the Americans, their embassy would be in danger. Taylor made a plan. He contacted the American CIA and let them know that he had six of their people. He also contacted his own government in Ottawa, Canada.

Taylor arranged for fake Canadian passports to be made for the six Americans. They had to be delivered in person by a Canadian courier because they couldn't trust the Iranian mail system. They also forged Iranian exit and entrance visas.

American CIA agent Antonio Mendez worked with the Canadian government and concocted a story that was almost unbelievable. He was going to pose as an American filmmaker who was scouting out a place to film his new science fiction movie, *Argo*.

> The CIA printed up posters to advertise the fake film. They made up a Hollywood film company and got elaborate costumes to disguise the Americans.

The CIA printed up posters to advertise the fake film. They made up a Hollywood film company and got elaborate costumes to disguise the Americans. Ads were placed in Hollywood magazines and a film party was held at a nightclub in Los Angeles. They even selected a real script based on a novel called *Lord of Light*. They did everything they could to make the cover believable.

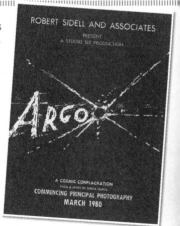

The American refugees were each given a secret identity with a backstory they had to memorize in case they were questioned. They were also given new hairstyles, clothes, and make-up to help disguise them. Finally, the CIA made reservations for six on a Swiss Air flight out of Iran.

They also made back-up reservations on British Airways and Air France planes. Then on January 27, they made their daring escape.

Disguised in Hollywood-style clothes, with their fake passports, the six American refugees left the Canadian Embassy and made their way to the airport. They talked loudly about the film they were making and what it would be like to film in Iran. No one questioned them. They made it to the airport and waited for the plane. All the while, they kept talking about their new science fiction film and what a success it would be. To anyone listening, they sounded and looked like Hollywood filmmakers. Amazingly they all made it out on the first flight. None of the back-up flights were needed.

The Movie Version

The story of the fake film and daring escape was so unbelievable that Hollywood took a page from Tony Mendez's cover story, making two movies about the Canadian Caper. One was made in May of 1981 and another in 2012. The 2012 film was named *Argo* and won the Academy Award for Best Picture. There is some controversy about the *Argo* film because it is a fictionalized account and does not explain how important the Canadians were in helping the American refugees escape.

As soon as the Americans were safely out of the Canadian Embassy, Ambassador Taylor began closing it down. The Canadians felt it was unsafe for their people to remain in Iran. When the American public learned about the escape and how the ambassador had helped the Americans, Ken Taylor became a hero to the people of the United States. He was awarded the Congressional Gold Medal and was appointed to be the Canadian Consul-General in New York City. The Americans he hid for 2 1/2 months were home free and safe. On January 21, 1981, Iran released the other American hostages. They were in captivity for 444 days.

Girrmann Escape Group

The Berlin Wall sliced through lives just as it cut through the city. People in West Berlin knew their friends and family were trapped in a communist country with no way out. Students of the Free University were afraid for the safety of their friends who lived in East Berlin. They had been allowed to study at the West Berlin school before the wall went up. But after August 13, 1961, they were totally cut off from school and their friends.

Many of the East German students who studied at the Free University were in favor of a democratic society that allowed freedoms like voting. The totalitarian government of East Germany considered people who wanted individual freedoms and the right to vote to be enemies of the state.

The government assigned Stasi police to spy on the East Germans and often arrested and jailed them for crimes against the government. A crime against the government could be as simple as owning a camera or radio that was made in West Germany. It was also considered a crime to have books or reading material that were anticommunist.

West German students were afraid for the safety of their friends trapped behind the wall. They needed to figure out a way to help them escape from East Berlin. But how? The wall was guarded 24 hours a day. Special papers and passports were required to even visit the east side of Berlin. It was a huge risk, but the university students were determined to rescue their friends.

Three students, Detlef Girrmann, Dieter Thieme, and Bodo Köhler worked out a plan for how to help their friends escape. They called themselves the Girrmann Group and agreed to work only with partners whom they completely trusted and to keep the group small. They knew they had to watch out for spies who might pretend to want to help in the escape. If a spy infiltrated the group, then it would be a disaster.

First, they had to recruit a few friends who held foreign passports. They were the only people who were allowed to enter East Berlin. One of these students was Burkhart Veigel. He agreed to work as a runner for the escape group.

His job was to make contact with students in East Berlin. He would show his passport to the guards at the wall and would be allowed to walk or drive into East Berlin for a day trip. He had to have a cover story as to why he was visiting. He tried to keep it simple and as close to the truth as possible. He often said he was visiting one of his school friends to take them something they had left behind.

Once he was inside the wall, he would find the student and meet with him or her. Veigel had to be very careful about what he said. The Stasi police had spies everywhere. If they were caught, then they would both be arrested and tried. Viegel for being an escape organizer, and the student for "fleeing the republic."

Once Viegel was sure that the student was not a spy or someone who had been "turned" by the Stasi, he could give them information about the plans for escape to the west. Code words were given. The student was told that he or she would receive a phone call from "Uncle Max." The "uncle" would tell the student to listen to a certain radio program. The time of the program would be the time of the next meeting.

Once Viegel had delivered the information, he returned to West Berlin by showing his passport at the gate. The student was left to wait for the phone call. Viegel reported back to Detlef Girrmann and his partners, and they went to work.

Girrmann, Thieme, and Köhler became experts at forging passports. They had connections with many Western officials who were sympathetic to their cause and helped by obtaining blank passports from other countries. People from countries like Belgium and Denmark donated illegal passports because they remembered the need to escape from the Nazis just 20 years before. The passports had to be forged with information that was believable and would cause no suspicion when presented to a border guard.

Once the passports were ready, the day of the escape would be set. The Girrmann Group gave the escapee as little notice as possible. Usually the escapees were told on the day that they were leaving. It helped eliminate the possibility that the escaping student might accidentally give information to a spy.

Another runner would have to go back into East Germany to deliver the forged documents and help the student get on the train. The runner was told not to wait for the student more than 10 minutes. If the student didn't show up, he or she was to leave immediately and the Girrmann Group would try to contact the student at a later date.

Following this rule was important. Standing around, or loitering, in East Germany caught the attention of the Stasi Police and you could be arrested. Also if the student didn't show up, something may have happened to alert the police and the runner would be arrested.

If the student did show up, he or she was given the passport and a train ticket. The student would travel by train to the country on the passport. The runner did not board the train with the student, because he had to check back out at the Berlin Wall. Once the student was on the train, he had a long nervous ride to see if he could make it out of East Germany to the safety of a new homeland.

For several months, this method worked well, but the East Germans began to notice that they were still losing people from East Berlin. They became stricter about checking passports and would detain anyone they thought might be trying to escape. Some of these were actual students the Girrmann Group was helping. Under heavy interrogation and imprisonment, some of the students told the Stasi about the Girrmann Group.

Viegel could no longer act as a runner for the group because he was put on a list of the most wanted citizens and a warrant was issued for his arrest. The leaders of East Germany accused the Girrmann Group of being terrorist "saboteurs" and enemies of the state.

Being discovered didn't stop the Girrmann Group— they just worked on new ideas for how to get people out of

East Berlin. They had to figure out ways to smuggle humans past the border guards and came up with several ideas. They learned how to build secret compartments in old cars. They would hide escapees under car seats and in false bottoms of trunks. They did whatever they could to help people escape the Stasi police and communist Germany.

It is estimated that from 1961 to 1963, the Girrmann Group helped 5,000 people escape from East Germany and start new lives in West Germany. By 1964, the Stasi police had managed to infiltrate the Girrmann Group, and Girrmann was declared Public Enemy Number One of East Berlin. Girrmann knew he had to stop, because if he was caught it could also put the people who worked with him in danger. But even though Girrmann had to "retire" from his work, there were others who were now trained and able to help the East Germans escape.

SPY TRAINING

Carrot Submarine

Materials:

- ❏ Paring knife
- ❏ Flat-bladed screwdriver (blade should be a little wider than a pencil)
- ❏ Pencil
- ❏ Big bowl of water (at least 3 inches deep)
- ❏ Carrot (ready-to-eat baby carrot)
- ❏ Several toothpicks
- ❏ Baking powder (not baking soda)

Cut the carrot in half—lengthwise. Use the screwdriver to drill a hole almost all the way through the carrot, from the flat side. The hole will be the bottom of your submarine. On top of the submarine, place four toothpicks: two on the top front and two on the top back.

Check out your submarine in the bowl of water. The sub should just barely sink below the surface. Add or remove toothpicks until it barely sinks.

Dry the carrot off and fill the hole with baking powder. Pack it in as tight as you can. Now your submarine is ready to launch. Watch it dive and surface and dive again.

If you need help with this activity, watch this video on YouTube: https://www.youtube.com/watch?v=7jqbEHsFly8

SPY TRAINING

Glaciers Move

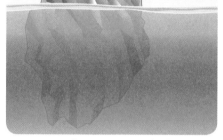

Project Iceworm didn't work because scientists underestimated the destructive power of moving glaciers. Glaciers move constantly, but as humans we think it takes a long time. You can demonstrate what happens when glaciers move by making glacier goo.

Materials:

- ☐ Two 8 oz. bottles of white glue
- ☐ Box of Borax powder
- ☐ Warm water
- ☐ Blue food coloring
- ☐ Two mixing bowls
- ☐ Spoon
- ☐ Measuring cup
- ☐ Cookie sheet

Empty one bottle of glue into the mixing bowl. Then fill the empty bottle with warm water. Shake it to get the rest of the glue to dissolve and then empty the bottle into the bowl. Mix together. Add 1/2 cup warm water to the glue. Then start spooning Borax into the glue. Keep stirring as you add more Borax. You will feel it start to turn to putty. You will need to keep adding Borax solution until all of the glue has a putty-like consistency. Set that batch aside.

Repeat using the next bottle of glue, but this time, add blue food coloring *before* you add the Borax. When you are finished, you will have white glacier goo and blue glacier goo.

Now you are ready to demonstrate how a glacier moves. Take the cookie sheet and prop it up on some books so that you have an inclined plane. Place both blobs of glacier goo at the top of the cookie sheet and let them flow down the sheet. This is how a glacier moves. You can see how the ice bumps and blends by how the two colors meld together.

Secret Weapons

TOP SECRET

East German T-72M was called the "monkey model" and had thinner armor and downgraded weapons systems, presented in a 1984 parade

Gadgets and Gizmos

You've seen the spy movies. James Bond is trapped by the evil villain and has to use one of his spy gadgets to save himself. Will he use the tear gas hidden in the can of powder or will he use one of the knives hidden in his shoe? They are all just movie props, nothing real, right?

Wrong!

During the Cold War, inventors on both sides of the conflict used newly discovered technology to equip their spies with tools right out of a movie. The race to get rockets and satellites into space resulted in the development of strong lightweight metals and plastics that could be used to make all sorts of new spy gadgets.

Mini cameras were popular with CIA agents, German Stasi agents, and the KGB. Spies hid the tiny cameras behind their neckties, in their purses, and on their watches. Some even put cameras in the handles of walking sticks. The tiny cameras were used so frequently that anyone caught with a mini camera was immediately suspected of being a spy.

Not only were the cameras special, but so was the film. When spies photographed the documents, the image was shrunken to a circle only one millimeter in diameter. The dot of film was then placed in a typed letter or under a stamp for the fellow spy to receive. These were called *microdots*, and they were a primary means of spy communication during the Cold War.

Spies also needed secret hiding places and gadget inventors went to work. They designed cufflinks that had a secret compartment to hide microfilm and hollow coins to hold messages or film. They even used the heels of shoes as secret compartments to hide information or tracking devices.

Besides disguising cameras, spies also wanted to hide their weapons and the gadget makers obliged. Personal objects that a spy would naturally carry were turned into weapons.

Don't Step There!

It may have looked like dog poop, but it was actually a radio transmitter. Agents could safely place the poop-shaped transmitter anywhere outside and nobody bothered it. The transmitter inside could be used to send messages or it could be a homing beacon to direct missiles to their target. It was one disguise that nobody wanted to touch to see if it was real or not.

That way, when the spies pulled out a pen or umbrella, no one would suspect they were ready to defend themselves.

Tiny pistols were designed to be hidden on the inside of a glove. The spy could defend himself without even taking off his mittens! A 4.5 mm single shotgun was disguised as a tube of lipstick and a 4 mm gun was made to look like a cigarette lighter.

Even an umbrella could be turned into a deadly weapon. Known as the Bulgarian umbrella, the harmless looking parasol actually hid a pneumatic mechanism for injecting small poisonous pellets of ricin under the victim's skin. It was successfully used by a Bulgarian agent to assassinate dissident writer, Georgi Markov.

Markov was walking across the Waterloo Bridge in London when he felt a sharp sting on the back of his right thigh. He turned around and saw a man picking an umbrella up off the ground. The man and the umbrella disappeared into a taxi. Markov went on to his job at the BBC World Service and told his coworkers about the strange incident. Later that day, he noticed what looked like a bug bite where he had felt the pain. That night he developed a fever and died 4 days later from ricin poisoning.

Less lethal but quite amazing is the CIA invention of a Dragonfly Insectothopter. This tiny unmanned aerial vehicle was developed in the 1970s and was to be used a surveillance tool. The insectothopter looked so real that it could buzz by people's heads (they might even swat at it) and they would never suspect that the dragonfly was actually spying on them.

These are just some of the tricks and tools that spy masters designed for their agents. Many spy devices are still considered top secret and cannot be revealed to the public. But if the spies could imagine it, the gadget makers could probably make it.

TOP SECRET
Spy in the Sky

It went by different code names. First it was called "Fulcrum," then it was the "Hexagon Project," but many people simply called it "Big Bird." It was a top-secret satellite that the United States started building in 1966, and it gave America the power to spy on the Soviet Union from 370 nautical miles above Earth.

The engineers recruited to build the top-secret satellite were sworn to secrecy. They couldn't tell their families what they were working on or where they were traveling. Sometimes the engineers would disappear for days at a time, and they could never explain where or why they were gone.

What they were making was the most sophisticated camera on the planet. It was far better than anything the Soviets had. Some engineers bragged that it could snap the picture of a license plate of any car parked at the Kremlin (Soviet headquarters).

The huge reconnaissance satellite weighed 7,375 pounds, and it was as big as a school bus. It carried 60 miles of film and four film return capsules. It was made of two huge cameras that worked together to produce very large panoramic pictures. One frame of the Hexagon's camera could show an expanse of the Earth from Washington, DC, to Cincinnati, OH. These pictures were so detailed that U.S. intelligence officers were able to see where the Soviets were building new bases or testing new equipment. It was far better than any spy plane because the Soviets could not shoot it down.

The Hexagon satellite could stay in space for up to 9 months, taking pictures the whole time. Every couple of months, the satellite would release a packet of film in a specially designed "re-entry" bucket that had a parachute. As the bucket floated back into the atmosphere, U.S. military aircraft would retrieve the film bucket with a grappling hook and deliver the film to the waiting scientists.

There were 19 successful launches of Hexagon satellites from 1971 to 1986. Hexagon provided nearly 100 miles of spy film and gave the U.S. military a perfect view of Soviet military movements. The Hexagon program was retired after 1986 in favor of new digital spy satellites that could relay the images directly to the ground stations for analysis.

Take Shelter

Sixth-grade students crouch under or beside their desks along with their teacher, 1951

The children were working on their math problems and the teacher was checking papers when the sirens blared. No one screamed or cried. The children calmly put down their pencils and crawled under their desks. They clasped their hands over their heads and waited for the teacher to tell them when they could move. It was a nuclear bomb drill, and during the 1950s, it was a regular occurrence in schools across America.

Any American school child could tell you exactly what to do in case of an atomic bomb—duck and cover. There was even a movie made by the Federal Civil Defense Administration to educate school children. It starred Bert the Turtle, and he taught the children that they would be safe as long as they would duck and cover.

Unfortunately that was not true. Scientists realized that the radioactive fallout from a nuclear bomb blast would kill just as many people as the initial blast. But government officials also knew that they had to protect the public from panic, so they decided to teach people the best methods they knew of to protect themselves.

The government selected special sites as "fallout shelters." These were usually basements in government or private businesses and were marked with a yellow and black nuclear symbol. Whole cities conducted fallout drills with sirens going off and people leaving their work to go to the basements of buildings. The government also stocked the shelters with supplies such as food, medical kits, flashlights, drinking water, and canned goods.

Individual families were told to "be prepared" and were given booklets that explained what to do in case of a nuclear attack. The government recommended that every family have a plan in place for where to go during the attack. Hiding in the basement was considered a good idea, but it was even better if you could afford to build a family bomb shelter.

Duck and Cover
You can watch the original movie of Bert the Turtle and see what children of the Cold War were taught in school at this link: http://www.youtube.com/watch?v=IKqXu-5jw60

Sheltered in Switzerland

Switzerland had the most nuclear fallout shelters of any country in the world—enough to house its entire population. To this day, it is a law in Switzerland that property owners must have a "protected place" and all apartments must be outfitted with shelters. Switzerland may be neutral in war, but it's definitely pro fallout shelter protection.

The Civil Defense Administration provided free plans for making your own bomb shelter. A simple shelter could be built in your existing basement with concrete blocks. An above ground shelter could be constructed in the backyard with double reinforced concrete. For the ultimate shelter, you could purchase a premade metal bunker that would be buried in the backyard. The family would have to climb down a hatch into the underground shelter.

Some fallout shelters were quite elaborate and had their own toilet, generator, and air ventilation system. All of the shelters had to be equipped with at least 2 weeks' worth of food and water, plus a battery-powered radio so families could hear the emergency broadcast system give instructions.

The handbook instructed people to stay completely inside the shelter for 2 weeks. They would then be allowed to be outside of the shelter for 3–4 hours a day but should continue to sleep in the shelter for several months. It was also

Children clutched their hands around their heads and necks to protect them against an atomic bomb, 1951

recommended that they take 130 mg of potassium oxide every day to protect their thyroid glands from radiation poisoning.

Fortunately, the Cold War ended without anyone setting off a nuclear bomb. The fallout shelters became playhouses for children or storage for lawn chairs and tools. Some of the underground shelters were covered over with dirt and simply forgotten.

In recent years, some new homeowners have been surprised to discover shelters hidden in their backyard. One man in Texas found a shelter that had been closed for 50 years. When he pried open the metal door, he found shelves stocked with 50-year-old peanut butter, crackers, and soup. He decided to clean up the old fallout shelter and now maintains it as a museum to show people the history of the Cold War.

The Thing

Most of the world never heard of Vadim Fedorovich Goncharov, and he wanted it that way. Goncharov was not just a secret agent for the KGB, but he was also a gadget inventor. He was an expert in cryptology (codes and code breaking), communications interception (listening devices), and optics (spy glasses).

His code name was Gorelov and he was the chief scientific and technical consultant of the KGB. He oversaw the invention of many gadgets for spy use. One of the most successful was called "The Thing." Originally invented by Léon Theremin as an electronic musical device that used two antennas to make sound, Goncharov saw the possibility of using the theremin as a spy tool. With alterations, the theremin could pick up sounds in a room and transmit those sounds to a receiver without the need for any wires.

Wireless sound detection was a totally new technology. This was a revolution in the spy world. Old wired technology made it difficult to hide a listening device. But this new Thing was amazing. It could be made very small so that it could be put anywhere. The gadget makers at the KGB got busy designing new objects that could hold The Thing. They created ashtrays, cigarette lighters, and decorative figurines. They wanted to use everyday objects that people would not suspect and that could stay in a room for a long period of time.

During the 1950s and 1960s, many people smoked cigarettes and ashtrays were in almost every living room and in many public lobbies. The spies would replace the normal ashtray with the KGB ashtray, making them able to listen to any conversation that happened in the room.

> Wireless sound detection was a totally new technology. This was a revolution in the spy world. Old wired technology made it difficult to hide a listening device.

Small ornamental statues or figurines could be given as a seemingly innocent gift. The recipient would place the figurine on a shelf and the spies would be able to hear conversations through it. This was especially effective for diplomats. Dignitaries who visited the Soviet embassy or the Kremlin would often receive the gift of a statue. Upon returning home, the dignitary would feel obligated to display the gift on a shelf in his or her office. Immediately the KGB had access to conversations in foreign offices.

Goncharov instructed KGB spies to place The Thing in rooms of Soviet hotels where Western visitors stayed. This gave the KGB access to conversations of anyone who visited from other countries.

He even figured out a way to listen to the conversations of the British royal family by having a Thing planted inside Princess Margaret's cigarette case and lighter. He also had the ashtrays fitted with the listening devices. For years, the KGB could listen in on the royal family whenever they wanted.

One of his greatest accomplishments was to place a Thing in the U.S. Ambassador's office. Goncharov cleverly planned for a group of Russian school children to visit the ambassador's office. The children sang patriotic songs and then gave the U.S. Ambassador a giant wooden seal of the United States of America. Of course the American Ambassador had to honor the gift from the children, so he had the seal hung on the wall in his office where everyone could see it.

> For years, the KGB could listen in on the royal family whenever they wanted.

That was exactly what Goncharov had hoped would happen. Inside the beak of the eagle on the great seal was a Thing. For 7 years, the KGB was able to listen to all of the conversations in that office. Neither the ambassador, nor any of his staff, ever suspected they had been a victim of the gadget guru, Goncharov.

Space Needles

Before the invention of satellites, all international communications were sent through undersea cables or bounced off the Earth's natural ionosphere. The cables provided excellent and reliable communication. The ionosphere was much less reliable and at times didn't work at all. This made the U.S. military quite worried. What if the Soviet Union managed to cut the undersea cables? The United States could be attacked and would not be able to communicate with its allies. It could be a disaster.

In 1963, military scientists decided to try to fix the problem by launching 480 million tiny copper needles into orbit around the Earth. The scientists hoped that the needles would create a ring that would circle the entire globe. It would be an artificial ionosphere that would be more reliable than the natural ionosphere and could be used for communication. The project was code named West Ford, and it was somewhat successful.

The first launch of the needles was unsuccessful, but on May 9, 1963, the second launch worked perfectly. The military sent a 40-pound package of copper needles in to space. The needles were densely packed in a block of naphthalene gel that would evaporate in space. In 2 months, the needles would spread out until their orbit would cover the entire Earth. By July, there was a doughnut-shaped cloud of copper needles 9 feet wide and 18 feet thick floating around the Earth. The needles were only 7/10 of an inch long. They were designed

Moon Bomb

Scientists came up with some wild ideas during the Cold War, but one of the craziest was to bomb the moon. Some U.S. scientists thought that if they exploded an atomic bomb on the moon, then it would scare the Soviet Union. The project was researched in the late 1950s and was called Project A119. Other scientists argued that a mistake could seriously hurt the Earth and ruin the surface of the moon. The plan was scrapped and no bombs were ever sent to the moon.

to create strong reflections when microwaves hit them so they would act like a tiny antenna.

The first communication trials were a success. Scientists used microwave dish antennas to send voice transmissions from California to Massachusetts. But as the needles spread out in space, the communication failed to work. Scientists believed if they sent up a cloud that was full of more needles, then they could make the project successful.

But the idea of a manmade cloud of copper needles worried other scientists. What problems would the needles cause for the Earth? It was a risk the scientists were not willing to take. The needles that had been sent to outer space were designed to slowly fall back to Earth after a few years. A thicker cloud might stay forever. The project was scrapped, and scientists instead worked to create the satellite communication systems we use today.

UFOs

The first report came on June 24, 1947. Private pilot Kenneth Arnold had seen nine strange objects flying in a line over Mount Rainier, WA. He said they were bright metallic bodies shaped like disks or saucers, and they flew incredibly fast.

Amazed by what he had seen, Arnold told his story to the local newspapers, and within a few days, the entire United States was talking about flying saucers and invasions from outer space.

But that wasn't the only sighting of strange objects flying in the sky. Hundreds of other people reported seeing strange lights in the night sky and fast-moving metal objects. Then in July of that same year came bizarre reports of a flying disc that had crash-landed near Roswell, NM. People were curious. What was going on? Were there really little green men invading from space? Or was there a more logical, military explanation?

For decades, people have speculated about a military installation called Area 51. Some people believed it was where the United States military was hiding the aliens that had crash-landed on Earth. Other people thought it was probably a test site for experimental military aircraft. In 2013, the U.S. government finally confirmed that Area 51 had been and still is a testing facility. And the strange flying objects were indeed ultra-fast super top secret planes.

Located by Groom Lake, NV, this salt flat was originally used by the U.S. Air Force during World War II. Those two airstrips eventually grew to multiple landing fields and several buildings—all classified

> For decades, people have speculated about a military installation called Area 51. Some people believed it was where the United States military was hiding the aliens that had crash-landed on Earth.

as top secret. The people who work in Area 51 are sworn to secrecy and can only talk about projects that have been declassified.

One such project is the U-2 program. This is quite possibly one of the experimental aircraft that people saw and reported as flying saucers. The U-2 was designed and built by Lockheed Martin and was tested at Area 51.

After WWII ended, it became apparent that the Soviet Union was a political opponent of the United States and its allies. Leaders of the U.S. decided they needed information on the military movements in the Soviet Union, so they began flying spy missions. The Soviets responded by shooting down several of the planes. The U.S. decided its best option was to build a plane that could fly so high the Soviet Union guns couldn't reach it.

> Leaders of the U.S. decided they needed information on the military movements in the Soviet Union, so they began flying spy missions.

That plane became the U-2. It could fly at the unbelievable altitude of 70,000 feet. Most planes of the 1950s could not exceed 45,000 feet. And the U.S. military believed that the Soviet antiaircraft missiles could not reach more than 48,000 feet.

Launched in 1955, the U-2 flew numerous missions and returned with very detailed photographs of military bases and airfields. When it was detected on Soviet radar, the U.S. said that it was really a craft used for high altitude weather research. President Dwight D. Eisenhower was worried that if the Soviets learned about the U.S. spy plane, there could be a war.

Scientists assured the President that it was impossible for the Soviets to shoot down the plane and there was minimal risk of the Soviets ever learning what they were doing.

But in May of 1960, the Soviet Union tracked the U-2 on radar and fired missiles at the plane. The U-2 crashed and the pilot was captured. President Eisenhower had to admit to Soviet leader Nikita Khrushchev that the U.S. had indeed been spying. The shooting of the U-2 spy plane led to the development of spy satellites that could not be shot down.

All of this work was top secret. Launching and testing experimental aircraft designed to keep the U.S. safe was important. It was also important to keep it a secret, so the stories of UFOs were allowed to persist. The government thought that it was better for civilians to daydream about flying saucers than to know about the real secrets of Area 51.

Flying Saucer 101

It's easy to make your own flying saucer.

Materials:

- ❑ Two paper plates
- ❑ Scissors
- ❑ Clear shipping tape
- ❑ Markers

Decorate the bottoms of the paper plates. This will be the exterior of your flying saucer so make it look good! After you have decorated them, turn the plates right side up and cover the plate with the shipping tape so that it has a smooth plastic surface. Use scissors to cut the excess tape.

Then hold the plates together and cut a circle out of the center of each plate. Now place the plates together with the decorated sides facing out. Tape the plates together. Make sure the outer edges are secure. There you have it! Your own flying saucer. Now take it for a spin.

Your Own UFO

UFO stands for "unidentified flying object." Often UFOs are strange and mysterious, but in reality, anything that can't be identified and is flying is a UFO. You can make a cool-looking UFO with just a straw and some paper.

Materials:

- ❏ A drinking straw
- ❏ Tape
- ❏ Scissors

- ❏ A 3 x 5 index card or piece of stiff paper

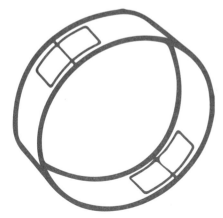

Cut three strips that measure 1 inch by 5 inches from the paper or index card. Take two of the strips and tape them together end to end. Then tape the long strip together to form a hoop.

Use the remaining strip of paper to make a smaller hoop. Tape the hoops to each end of the straw. The straw should be lined up on the inside of the hoops.

That's all there is to it! You are ready to launch your UFO and watch it fly.

Children in West Berlin climb the wall to look over the other side to East Berlin in 1961

Books

Funder, A. (2011). *Stasiland: Stories from behind the Berlin Wall.* New York, NY: Harper Perennial.

Gadchick. (2012). *Sex, spies, gadgets, and secrets: The women of the Cold War.* Seattle, WA: CreateSpace & Author.

Macrakis, K. (2008). *Seduced by secrets: Inside the Stasi's spy-tech world.* New York, NY: Cambridge University Press.

Melton, H. K., & Wallace, R. (2009). *The official CIA manual of trickery and deception.* New York, NY: HarperCollins.

Ozorak, P. (2013). *Underground structures of the Cold War: The world below.* South Yorkshire, England: Pen and Sword Military.

Sulick, M. J. (2013). *American spies: Espionage against the United States from the Cold War to the present.* Washington, DC: Georgetown University Press.

Taylor, F. (2007). *The Berlin Wall: A world divided 1961–1989.* New York, NY: Harper Perennial.

Websites

American Experience. (n.d.). *Race for the superbomb: First Soviet test.* Retrieved from http://www.pbs.org/wgbh/amex/bomb/peopleevents/pandeAMEX53.html

Associated Press. (2011). *Decades later, a Cold War secret is revealed.* Retrieved from http://www.foxnews.com/us/2011/12/26/decades-later-cold-war-secret-is-revealed/

Atomic age bomb shelter opened after 50 years. (2013). Retrieved from http://www.news.com.au/technology/design/atomic-age-bomb-shelter-opened-after-50-years/story-fnjwucti-1226758891412

The Baltic Initiative and Network. (n.d.). *The Glienicke Bridge or Bridge of Spies, Berlin.* Retrieved from http://coldwarsites.net/country/germany/the-glienicke-bridge-or-bridge-of-spies-berlin/

Barnett, A. (2000). US planned one big nuclear blast for mankind. *The Guardian.* Retrieved from http://www.theguardian.com/science/2000/may/14/space exploration.theobserver

Benson, R. L. (n.d.). *The Venona Story.* Center for Cryptologic History, National Security Agency. Retrieved from https://www.nsa.gov/about/_files/cryptologic_heritage/publications/coldwar/venona_story.pdf

Blumenthal, R. (1994). A graying onetime double agent returns to scenes of old intrigue. *The New York Times.* Retrieved from http://www.nytimes.com/1994/07/17/us/a-graying-onetime-double-agent-returns-to-scenes-of-old-intrigue.html?src=pm&pagewanted=1

Carle, M. (n.d.). Operation Ivy Bells. *Military.com.* Retrieved from http://www.military.com/Content/MoreContent1/?file=cw_f_ivybells

CBSNews.com. (2010). *A look back at America's fallout shelter fatuation.* Retrieved from http://www.cbsnews.com/news/a-look-back-at-americas-fallout-shelter-fatuation/

Childs, D. (2011). Detlef Girrmann: Lawyer who helped hundreds of students escape from East Germany. *The Independent.* Retrieved from http://www.independent.co.uk/news/obituaries/detlef-girrmann-lawyer-who-helped-hundreds-of-students-escape-from-east-germany-2308725.html

Crossland, D. (2011). The tunnel digger: Escapee reveals sweet revenge against East German regime. *Spiegel Online.* Retrieved from http://www.spiegel.de/international/germany/the-tunnel-digger-escapee-recalls-sweet-revenge-against-east-german-regime-a-779231.html

Edwards, M. (2001). The sphinx and the spy. *Genii: The Conjuror's Magazine.* Retrieved from http://www.frankolsonproject.org/Articles/Mulholland.html

Escaping the East by any means. (2009). *Aljazeera.* Retrieved from http://www.aljazeera.com/focus/2009/10/200910793416112389.html

Farndale, N. (2011). Double-O who? Meet history's unsung spies. *The Telegraph.* Retrieved from http://www.telegraph.co.uk/history/world-war-two/8749894/Double-O-Who-Meet-historys-unsung-spies.html

Fitsanakis, J. (2012). *Fascinating profile of the Soviet KGB's little-known tech wizard.* Retrieved from http://intelnews.org/2012/12/24/01-1161/#more-9753

Floorwalker, M. (2013). 10 ridiculous Cold War government projects. *ListVerse.* Retrieved from http://listverse.com/2013/03/20/10-ridiculous-cold-war-government-projects/

Foreign Affairs, Trade and Development Canada. (2013). *Ken Taylor and the Canadian caper.* Retrieved from http://international.gc.ca/history-histoire/people-gens/ken_taylor.aspx?lang=eng

Grenoble, R. (2013). 'Secret' nuclear missile launch code during Cold War was '00000000.' *Huffington Post.* Retrieved from http://www.huffingtonpost.com/2013/12/05/nuclear-missile-code-00000000-cold-war_n_4386784.html

Grigonis, R. (2013). Spy tools: 15 strange surveillance devices of the Cold War. *Newsmax.* Retrieved from http://www.newsmax.com/TheWire/spy-surveillance-cold-war-tools/2013/11/01/id/534386/

Guillemette, R. (2011). Declassified US spy satellites reveal rare look at secret Cold War space program. *Space.com.* Retrieved from http://www.space.com/12996-secret-spy-satellites-declassified-nro.html

Hall, A. (2011). *Wall that divided the world.* Retrieved from http://www.express.co.uk/expressyourself/264722/Wall-that-divided-the-world

Hawkings, D. (2004). Blue peacock: The army's forgotten weapon. *Discovery: The Science and Technology Journal of AWE.* Retrieved from http://www.joe-ks.com/archives_apr2004/BluePeacock.pdf

Hirschson, Y. M. (2012). Espionage: The unknown spies: Boris Yuzhin. *Zman Magazine.* Retrieved from http://www.zmanmagazine.com/PDF/Espionage%20Boris%20Yuzhin.pdf

History.com. (n.d.). *Berlin Wall.* Retrieved from http://www.history.com/topics/cold-war/berlin-wall

Howell, E. (2012). Sputnik: The space race's opening shot. *Space.com.* Retrieved from http://www.space.com/17563-sputnik.html

Kendall, A. (2006). Earth's artificial ring: Project West Ford. *DamnInteresting.com.* Retrieved from http://www.damninteresting.com/earths-artificial-ring-project-west-ford/

Layton, J. (2006). How can you train honeybees to sniff for bombs? *HowStuffWorks.com.* Retrieved from http://science.howstuffworks.com/bomb-sniffing-bees.htm

Leskovitz, F. J. (n.d.). *Camp Century, Greenland.* Retrieved from http://gombessa.tripod.com/scienceleadstheway/id9.html

Manaugh, G. (2011). Project Iceworm: The nuclear city hidden under Greenland's glaciers. *BLDGBLOG.* Retrieved from http://io9.com/5740188/project-iceworm-the-nuclear-city-hidden-under-greenlands-glaciers

Melita Norwood [Obituary]. (2005). *The Telegraph.* Retrieved from http://www.telegraph.co.uk/news/obituaries/1492969/Melita-Norwood.html

NASA. (2007). *Sputnik: The fiftieth anniversary.* Retrieved from http://history.nasa.gov/sputnik/

National Geographic. (n.d.). *Area 51's secrets.* Retrieved from http://natgeotv.com.au/tv/area-51s-secrets/

NebraskaStudies.org. (n.d.). *The family fallout shelter.* Retrieved from http://www.nebraskastudies.org/0900/frameset_reset.html?http://www.nebraskastudies.org/0900/stories/0901_0132.html

Peter Lunn [Obituary]. (2011). *The Telegraph.* Retrieved from http://www.telegraph.co.uk/news/obituaries/military-obituaries/special-forces-obituaries/8939098/Peter-Lunn.html

Rice, L. (n.d.). 4 awesome NASA inventions you use everyday. *Curiosity.com.* Retrieved from http://www.discovery.com/tv-shows/curiosity/topics/ten-nasa-inventions.htm

Royal Air Force Museum. (n.d.). *The Cambridge Four.* Retrieved from http://www.nationalcoldwarexhibition.org/schools-colleges/national-curriculum/espionage/the-cambridge-four.aspx

Ruck, A. (2010). Thinker, author, skier, spy. *Ski+board.* Retrieved from http://www.skiclub.co.uk/assets/files/documents/skihero.pdf

Science Bob. (n.d.). *The incredible hoop glider.* Retrieved from http://www.sciencebob.com/experiments/straw_hoop_plane.php

Smith, C. (2007). Spy Robert Schaller's life of secrecy, betrayal and regrets. *Seattle PI.* Retrieved from http://www.seattlepi.com/local/article/Spy-Robert-Schaller-s-life-of-secrecy-betrayal-1232285.php

Snow, J. (2010). Le Carré betrayed by 'bad lot' spy Kim Philby. *Channel 4 News.* Retrieved from http://www.channel4.com/news/articles/uk/le+carr233+betrayed+by+aposbad+lotapos+spy+kim+philby/3766077.html

Spartacus Educational. (n.d.). *Kim Philby.* Retrieved from http://spartacus-educational.com/SSphilby.htm

SpyMuseum.com. (n.d.). *Great seal bug.* Retrieved from http://spymuseum.com/dt_portfolio/great-seal-bug/

Strickland, J., & Kiger, P. J. (2007). How Area 51 works. *HowStuffWorks.com.* Retrieved from http://science.howstuffworks.com/space/aliens-ufos/area-51.htm

Tallman. (2003). *Operation Ivy Bells.* Retrieved from http://everything2.com/title/Operation+Ivy+Bells

Taylor, F. (2007). The Berlin Wall: A secret history. *History Today, 57*(2). Retrieved from http://www.historytoday.com/frederick-taylor/berlin-wall-secret-history

Trex, E. (2011). 8 creative ways people went over the Berlin Wall. *Mental Floss.* Retrieved from http://mentalfloss.com/article/28517/8-creative-ways-people-went-over-berlin-wall

Tweedle, N. (2013). Kim Philby: Father, husband, traitor, spy. *The Telegraph.* Retrieved from http://www.telegraph.co.uk/history/9818727/Kim-Philby-Father-husband-traitor-spy.html

US planned to nuke the moon. (2012). *The Sydney Morning Herald.* Retrieved from http://www.smh.com.au/technology/sci-tech/us-planned-to-nuke-the-moon-20121128-2aejm.html

Vanderbilt, T. (2013). The CIA's most highly trained spies weren't even human. *Smithsonian Magazine.* Retrieved from http://www.smithsonianmag.com/history/the-cias-most-highly-trained-spies-werent-even-human-20149/

War History Online. (2014). *It's true: T-1151 dog doo transmitter.* Retrieved from http://www.warhistoryonline.com/war-articles/true- t-1151-dog-doo-transmitter.html

Web Urbanist. (n.d.). *Weird military inventions: 10 crazy weapons of war.* Retrieved from http://weburbanist.com/2010/01/12/weird-military-innovations/

Wellerstein, A. (2012). *Rare photos of the Soviet bomb project.* Retrieved from http://blog.nuclearsecrecy.com/2012/07/27/rare-photos-of-the-soviet-bomb-project/

Wikipedia. (n.d.). *Berlin Wall.* Retrieved from http://en.wikipedia.org/wiki/Berlin_Wall

Wikipedia. (n.d.). *Elizabeth Bentley.* Retrieved from http://en.wikipedia.org/wiki/Elizabeth_Bentley

Wikipedia. (n.d.). *Igor Kurchatov.* Retrieved from http://en.wikipedia.org/wiki/Igor_Kurchatov

Wikipedia. (n.d.). *Screw-propelled vehicle.* Retrieved from http://en.wikipedia.org/wiki/Screw-propelled_vehicle

Wikipedia. (n.d.). *Soviet atomic bomb project.* Retrieved from http://en.wikipedia.org/wiki/Soviet_atomic_bomb_project

Woollaston, V. (2013). Cameras disguised inside coat zips and bugs hidden in tree trunks: Fascinating insight into the crafty tricks and devious gadgets German spies used during the Cold War. *Daily Mail.* Retrieved from http://www.dailymail.co.uk/sciencetech/article-2423361/Crafty-tricks-devious-gadgets-German-spies-used-Cold-War-revealed.html

About the Author

Stephanie Bearce is a writer, a teacher, and a history detective. She loves tracking down spies and uncovering secret missions from the comfort of her library in St. Charles, MO. When she isn't writing or teaching, Stephanie loves to travel the world and go on adventures with her husband, Darrell.

More Books in This Series

TOP SECRET FILES

Stealthy spies, secret weapons, and special missions are just part of the mysteries uncovered when kids dare to take a peek at the *Top Secret Files*. Featuring books that focus on often unknown aspects of history, this series is sure to hook even the most reluctant readers, taking them on a journey as they try to unlock some of the secrets of our past.

Top Secret Files: The American Revolution

George Washington had his own secret agents, hired pirates to fight the British, and helped Congress smuggle weapons, but you won't learn that in your history books! Learn the true stories of the American Revolution and how spies used musket balls, books, and laundry to send messages. Discover the female Paul Revere, solve a spy puzzle, and make your own disappearing ink. It's all part of the true stories from the *Top Secret Files: The American Revolution*.

ISBN-13: 978-1-61821-247-4

Top Secret Files: The Civil War

The Pigpen Cipher, the Devil's Coffee Mill, and germ warfare were all a part of the Civil War, but you won't learn that in your history books! Discover the truth about Widow Greenhow's spy ring, how soldiers stole a locomotive, and the identity of the mysterious "Gray Ghost." Then learn how to build a model submarine and send secret light signals to your friends. It's all part of the true stories from the *Top Secret Files: The Civil War*.

ISBN-13: 978-1-61821-250-4

Top Secret Files: Gangsters and Bootleggers

Blind pigs, speakeasies, coffin varnish, and tarantula juice were all a part of the Roaring 20s. Making alcohol illegal didn't get rid of bars and taverns or crime bosses—they just went underground. Secret joints were in almost every large city. Discover the crazy language and secret codes of the Prohibition Era—why you should mind your beeswax and watch out for the gumshoe talking to the fuzz or you might end up in the cooler! It's all part of the true stories from the *Top Secret Files: Gangsters and Bootleggers*.

ISBN-13: 978-1-61821-461-4 • **Available October 2015**

Top Secret Files: Pirates and Buried Treasure

Julius Caesar was kidnapped by pirates and Sir Frances Drake was both a swashbuckler and a knight, plundering ships in the name of the British Crown, but you won't learn that in your history books! Discover the secrets of Calico Jack and Blackbeard, and how kung fu monks were hired to try to fight off pirates. Then learn how to talk like a pirate and make a buried treasure map for your friends. It's all part of the true stories from the *Top Secret Files: Pirate Ships and Buried Treasure.*

ISBN-13: 978-1-61821-421-8 • **Available August 2015**

Top Secret Files: The Wild West

Bandits, lawmen, six shooters, bank robberies, and cowboys were all a part of the Wild West. But so were camels, buried treasure, and gun-slinging dentists. Dive into strange tales like the mysterious Cave of Gold, filled with ancient skeletons, and Rattle Snake Dick's lost fortune. Discover the truth about notorious legends like Jesse James, Buffalo Bill, former spy-turned-bandit Belle Star, and Butch Cassidy and the Sundance Kid. Then, learn why it's unlucky to have a dead man's hand when playing cards and how to talk like a real cowpoke. It's all part of the true stories from the *Top Secret Files: The Wild West.*

ISBN-13: 978-1-61821-462-1 • **Available October 2015**

Top Secret Files: World War I

Flame throwers, spy trees, bird bombs, and Hell Fighters were all a part of World War I, but you won't learn that in your history books! Uncover long-lost secrets of spies like Howard Burnham, "The One Legged Wonder," and nurse-turned-spy, Edith Cavell. Peek into secret files to learn the truth about the Red Baron and the mysterious Mata Hari. Then learn how to build your own Zeppelin balloon and mix up some invisible ink. It's all part of the true stories from the *Top Secret Files: World War I.*

ISBN-13: 978-1-61821-241-2

Top Secret Files: World War II

Spy school, poison pens, exploding muffins, and Night Witches were all a part of World War II, but you won't learn that in your history books! Crack open secret files and read about the mysterious Ghost Army, rat bombs, and doodlebugs. Discover famous spies like the White Mouse, super-agent Garbo, and baseball player and spy, Moe Berg. Then build your own secret agent kit and create a spy code. It's all part of the true stories from the *Top Secret Files: World War II.*

ISBN-13: 978-1-61821-244-3